unequally yoked

WIVES

When a man is living with a Christian woman, he is marked for special treatment. A servant of God is living with him, sharing his meals and his bed. Think of that—a SPECIAL AGENT of the Lord is the closest person to him in the world. She's in a position to minister the Word to him without his being aware of it—IF SHE KNOWS HOW.

Many godly women, as you know, are begging God to SEND SOMEONE along to win their husbands. It's likely to be a long wait. That method is second best and God holds off on second best for a long time. No dear wife, God's method for reaching your unsaved husband is **YOU!**

I can almost hear the exclamation. . ."Dr. Lovett, you mean to say that God EXPECTS ME to win my husband?" That's exactly what I mean, dear sister. The Word is definite about it. Yet I know what you're thinking. You're wondering how a woman can be totally submissive to a man (as the Word teaches) and win him to the Lord at the same time. Well, God has provided a way and it is more powerful than you ever dreamed.

The reason I can say that is because I know the fabulous technique He has built into my book, **UNEQUALLY YOKED WIVES.** It was written for godly, submissive wives, who long to see their husbands saved—yet don't realize they are the ones God is waiting to use.

unequally yoked
WIVES

by

C. S. Lovett

M.A., B.D., D.D.

author of
**DEALING WITH THE DEVIL
JESUS WANTS YOU WELL!
SOUL-WINNING MADE EASY**

director of Personal Christianity

Published by

PERSONAL CHRISTIANITY
Baldwin Park, California 91706

PRINTED IN THE UNITED STATES OF AMERICA
by
EL CAMINO PRESS
La Verne, California 91750

1977

CONTENTS

C. S. Lovett . . .

the author is married to Marjorie.

After 35 years of marriage, both
agree God's plan for making two
people one is just great!

THE
NUTCRACKER TECHNIQUE

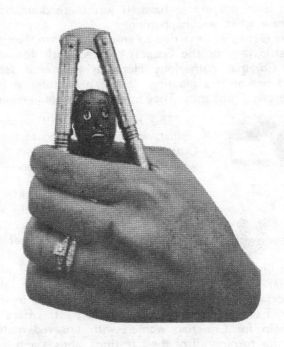

IN A NUTSHELL; this technique is a plan for taking all of the testings and trials, pressures and pain of being married to an unsaved man and using them SYSTEMATICALLY . . . **in the power of the Holy Spirit** . . . to bring him to Christ!

PREFACE

SHE'S HERE! SHE'S HERE!

Shouts of joy interrupted the meeting. People turned in their seats to watch. A lady hurried down the aisle. Excitement mounted as she reached a group of friends in the front row. Everything stopped while they embraced — and cried. They'd been praying so hard. It was quite dramatic. Everyone knew what was happening.

Mrs. Jones was married to an unsaved man. Not only was he hostile towards the Gospel, he frequently forbad her to attend Christian gatherings. Her praying friends desperately wanted her at this meeting. It was a conference for wives with unsaved husbands. They knew what it could mean to her.

 The husband, a well known industrialist, was fully exposed to the Gospel. Outstanding Christian leaders had dealt with him. But he was stubborn. At times, anything Christian triggered his rage. Friends often feared for Mrs. Jones' safety. They'd seen her on the receiving end of his tirades. But here she was, burdened with that ceaseless longing to see her husband saved.

An unusual case? My word, no. Thousands of wives face a similar situation. But it isn't Mrs. Jones or her story that is important to us here. It's what she CAN DO in the midst of it. That's the purpose of this book. It offers step by step help for Christian women with unsaved mates. It is a plan for turning all of their testings, abuses and sufferings around and using them for the salvation of their husbands.

The Apostle Paul was alert to these situations. He has spoken directly to this very matter:

"For the unbelieving husband is sanctified by his wife, and the unbelieving wife is sanctified by her believing husband. . . ."*

---

*1 Corinthians 7:14

8

How does that work?

When God beholds an unsaved man joined to one of His children, you can be sure that man is marked for **special treatment.** He is in for an unusual contact with the Gospel. Why? He is joined to a person in whom the Spirit of God lives. Imagine a pagan joined for life to someone who belongs to the Most High God! He's in contact with the reality of Christ. He lives with it — 24 hours a day!

That alone is sanctification of a wondrous sort. But there is more. The Christian wife is herself a "sanctifier." That is, she has a unique ministry to this man. Because of the marriage relationship, she is closer to him than anyone. She can reach him as no one else. You bet such a man is sanctified, for "sanctified" in this case means . . . "set apart for special treatment." God is ready to deal with this man in a marvelous way through the wife, if He can get the wife to be the "sanctifier" she ought to be.

Wait a minute! The home is a tough place for evangelism!

Right. I agree. Salvation is a matter better settled before people marry. Who wants to be tied to someone perpetually trying to convert him? It's easy to see how a pestered mate could become antagonistic toward the Gospel. But that only means a wife must learn how to approach her husband subtly — with skill — and a plan for working with the Holy Spirit.

Like it or not, the wife is called to be a "sanctifier" of her husband. That's what Paul is saying. Of all people she is the one God uses BEST for reaching that man. It's one thing, though, to believe Paul's word, quite another to WATCH IT WORK. That verse cannot be put into operation until the Christian wife learns the techniques and action steps for reaching her husband. Until she learns how to turn her ROLE AS A WIFE into an evangelistic opportunity, there can be no sanctification.

● Mrs. Jones came to the conference for the purpose of learning how to put that verse to work in her home. She was ready to become a sanctifying wife. She had the burden, but lacked the KNOW-HOW. She went away with the specific techniques and insights found in this manual. Today her husband is saved!

TOMORROW — YOURS?

Chapter One

GOD'S WEDDING DAY!

At the appointed hour the bells of heaven ring out the announcement:

> **"Let us be glad and rejoice and give all glory to Him, for the marriage of the Lamb is come and His bride has made herself ready"** (Rev. 19:7).

In that moment the Lord will say, "I, Jesus, take thee, Miss Church to be my eternally wedded wife." When the ceremony ends, you and I will be **full partners** with God in glory, fulfilling that Word which now calls us "joint heirs with Christ!" (Rom. 8:17). In an instant two become one! God intends every marriage to be like that, especially His own.

And what has He done to insure the success of His marriage?

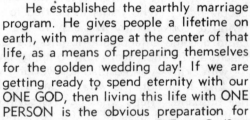

He established the earthly marriage program. He gives people a lifetime on earth, with marriage at the center of that life, as a means of preparing themselves for the golden wedding day! If we are getting ready to spend eternity with our ONE GOD, then living this life with ONE PERSON is the obvious preparation for it. Should not everyone prepare for marriage? Even God?

GOD'S MARITAL PREPARATIONS

Before the wedding plans were made, God had a serious problem. I'll ask you a question which brings that problem into instant focus:

> **"Have you ever thought of the awfulness of being a God of love with NO ONE to love?"**

That's what it was like before man was made. The Holy Spirit goes beyond describing our Heavenly Father as a loving God. He says, **"God is love!"** What does that mean? He has to love — **He can't help Himself** — it's His nature!

The fall has so damaged us we can't feel the fire of love with no one to love. We like ourselves too much for that. But that was God's predicament. That's why one of the earliest pronouncements says:

"Let us make man in our image and after our likeness."*

What else was God to do? Make some pets? Fashion zombies? Could He be satisfied with live models? Hardly. A God of love must have those who can RETURN HIS LOVE.

 They must be able to love Him just as He loved them. Nothing less than His own KIND can do that. Why should He settle for less. Could He be expected to coddle inferiors for all His days — without their being able to reciprocate? No. God needs people, not pets.

That is why you and I are His image. We are made no less than God's OWN KIND. We are designed to RECEIVE His love without limit and return it. What does it take to do this? What kind of a being is capable of embracing the FULNESS OF GOD — returning His love in equal measure? Answering that may cause you to revise your estimate of man. There is no way for anything less than God's OWN KIND to meet the longing of His heart.

● It was having no one to love that drove God into the people-business. But that's a business with risks. To make people capable of loving Him — as He longs to be loved — requires they be free. They must have the freedom of choice. If men are not entirely free, they can't be like Him at all. If they are not free, then neither is their response. Neither can they love, for love must be freely given, or it is not love.

If men are to love God as He yearns to be loved, then they must be able to GIVE their love — or WITHHOLD it. More is involved in producing free people than decreeing them into existence. God can't say, **"I would that my house be full of loving companions"** and get them. It can't be done. That would be like saying, **"I would that none should perish."** He can wish it all He likes, but is powerless to prevent it — and give men their freedom at the same time.

---

*Genesis 1:26

11

SO — once you bring freewill creatures into existence you need to test them. Why? To see what they will do with their freedom of choice. That's what the earthly program is all about. It is the story of God's proving ground and the testing of His image. But testing alone isn't enough. God wants more than proven people. He wants more than just His bare image. What then?

He wants people LIKE HIMSELF. That is the second major problem of the people-business. It isn't hard, you see, for God to reproduce Himself in free-will creatures and test them. But how will He get those creatures to THINK and ACT and FEEL as He does? That's His biggest problem. He can't decree it. But He does have a plan. He never would have started the whole thing if He didn't. Once we understand the plan, we see the pains God has taken to secure companions ready to spend their lives with Him — FOREVER!

WHY NOT IN HEAVEN?

Ever wonder why God chose **not** to produce His people in heaven? Why the program must be carried out on earth? The plain fact is, heaven is no place to raise kids. There is no way to produce God's likeness there. The conditions required for bringing people to maturity are not found there.

> **"And God shall wipe away all tears from their eyes; and there shall be no more death** (that's what scares people), **neither sorrow nor crying, neither shall there be any more pain:** (take that away and who cares about anything?): **for the former things are passed away"** (Rev. 21:4).

Wow! Doesn't that sound great! How blissful. Just think, no more stress or toil of any kind. Total relaxation! What blessedness you say? Yes. But unfortunately that's no way to raise children. You know what happens to children if you take away their stresses and shield them from the blows of life. It destroys them. Consequently, heaven is no place to bring sons to maturity. It would produce exactly the opposite God seeks. You've seen coddled kids, they're awful.

Put three toddlers in a crib. Set a toy in their midst. How long does it take for the grabbing and squalling to start? It's human nature to TAKE and HURT. Billy Graham is credited with saying, **"You don't have to teach children to be bad."** Who has to tell you how hard it is to build the sweeter graces in your children? What then, does it take to mould people into the likeness of the Lord. Anyone can see that it can't possibly happen overnight.

How then?

How does a man become long-suffering, for example? That's just one of the graces listed in Galatians. You recognize the answer — **by suffering a long time.** There's no short cut. Consider how one develops patience. That too is a divine grace. This is gained by enduring one anxiety situation after another. How about the wondrous grace of forgiveness. What does it take to become a forgiving person? You have to be hurt again and again and again. Does not one have to be hurt before he can forgive? Indeed.

 Well then, how much hurt is there in heaven? None you say? Then you would never forgive anyone there, would you? No. You couldn't learn forgiveness then? Could one become a patient person in a place where there is no anxiety? What about the strengths gained through resisting temptation? How can that be acquired in a place where there is none? Will there be any need there for holding temper and tongue? What is there about heaven that could make you a gentler person, when that grace is acquired through taking abuse?

See? It takes a lifetime of frustrations, sorrows and anguish for people to change into the likeness of the Lord. None of these is found in heaven. No, heaven is no place to bring up the children of God. That's what the earth is for. It alone provides the kind of a life needed to produce the divine personality. It is the laboratory of life that prepares us for the real life with God. It cannot be by-passed.

I could go on to show how each of the divine graces can only be produced through the experiences of this life alone.

That is why our earthly experience is God's ingenious method of preparing people to live with Him. The plan includes Adam too. He wasn't perfect, far from it. He was a very self-asserting man, for he decidedly preferred fellowship with his wife to God. He had a long way to go before he was ready for eternity — **even before the fall.** That simply manifested what was already in him.

THE LABORATORY OF MARRIAGE

With marriage at the center of life as we know it, it follows that it is also the central laboratory for making us like Christ. Here we find all the ingredients for Christlikeness. It is a complete lab with all of the stresses and trials, pressures and possibilities packaged under one roof. Everything needed to reproduce God's personality in us can be found in our homes. Marriage is a home-study course, an earthly rehearsal for the golden wedding to come.

Here, in an environment of stress and strain we learn to live exclusively for another person — our mate. Is it easy? Far from it. God never said it would be easy. Life on this earth is not easy. It is one of continual struggle and strife. If marriage is the center of this life, then it is at once the focal point of all our troubles. Marriage is the most stressful fact of life.

Now if you think that is a harsh view of earthly marriage, wait until you see what God thinks of it. You might be shocked. That's next.

14

Chapter Two

MARRIAGES ARE NOT MADE IN HEAVEN!

Who said so? Jesus.

He did it when answering a question put by a sect of the Jews who didn't believe in the resurrection — the Sadducees. They denied the existence of people in the spirit, refused any doctrine of angels and disavowed life apart from a physical body. Like some today, they said . . . "When you're dead, you're dead." So they set about to trap the Lord Jesus with a marital question. They asked:

> "Teacher, Moses wrote this law for us: 'If a man dies and leaves a wife, but no children, that man's brother must marry the widow so they can have children for the dead man.' 29. Once there were seven brothers; the oldest got married, and died without having any children. 30. Then the second one married the woman, 31. and then the third; the same thing happened to all seven — they died without having children. 32. Last of all, the woman died. 33. Now, on the day when the dead are raised to life, whose wife will she be? All seven of them had married her!" (Luke 20 Today's English Version)

Their question was full of sarcasm. Yet the Master was gracious. He stooped to answer. When He did, His reply exploded a bomb of insight concerning the matter of marriage in heaven:

> "People in this world," Jesus replied, "marry and are given in marriage. But those who are considered worthy of reaching that world, which means rising from the dead, neither marry nor are given in marriage. They cannot die any more but live like the angels . . ." (Luke 20:34-36a. J. B. Phillips trans.).

NO MARRIAGES IN HEAVEN!

The Sadducees never expected to hear Jesus say, **"There's no such thing as marriage in heaven,"** adding in the same breath, **"Angels live there too."** See how carefully He stated the fact of the two worlds, sharply dividing between, "This one" and "that one!" His answer to the Sadducees, who thought they had Him over a barrel with their proposition, brought out the startling truth that marriage is an earthly institution with no trace of it carried over into the next life.

Observe that He does not say we become angels in the next life. Only that we are LIKE THEM. In saying that the citizens of heaven "neither marry nor are given in marriage," He announces marriage is a condition of this life only. In fact, whenever Jesus is questioned about marriage, He always brings up the PHYSICAL nature of marriage, pointing out the sex-difference in bodies:

"Have ye not read that HE which made them at the beginning made them male and female?" (Matthew 19:4).

Once you say, "male" and "female" you are mentioning **animal bodies** with their differences in sex. While bodies may be classified by sex, the people inside those bodies cannot. They have no sex. Why? Spirit-beings are people without bodies. True, God does put them inside bodies for their earthly probation and those bodies may be either male or female. Therefore the body you are wearing now may identify you as a woman in this life. But in the life to come you will not be a woman. Why? You won't have this animal body there. It is physical, and heaven is life in the Spirit. They are two different worlds.

There will be neither male nor female in heaven. Those physical distinctions belong to the physical creation **alone.** Puzzled about that? It's not hard to satisfy yourself as to its truth.

Go to a funeral. Behold the body in the casket. It lies there complete—with its sexuality, brain and all. Yet something is obviously missing. What? The person! He's gone! The one who was inside that body has departed. He left everything physical behind. Where is he? If he were a Christian, he is with the Lord. For to be "absent from the body," is to be "present with the Lord."*

---

*2 Corinthians 5:8

Why would I send you to a funeral for such an observation? Who can look upon a dead body and argue that man is part body — when the fellow is obviously GONE! There is no personality to a corpse. That belongs to the person. There's no person inside a dead body.

The point. You and I are **not bodies** — we simply WEAR ONE for the time we are on earth. Bodies belong to the earth, having to do with this life only. They are "earth suits" which we must wear to participate in life on earth. This is what allows us to go through the laboratory of life as men — cut off from our natural habitat — **heaven!** You see, we were never designed to live on earth. Therefore a special device had to be provided so that we could have an existence away from our home in heaven. It is much like the deep sea diver who must don a **complete outfit** so that he can survive on the ocean's floor.

EARTHLY MARRIAGE—ONE FLESH

Marriage is based on bodies — and their differences in sex. Marriage partners are sexual opposites, coming together on the basis of this difference. The Lord Jesus always linked marriage to the difference in sex for after telling the Pharisees that God had placed His image in bodies, making them "male and female," He added:

> **"For this cause shall a man leave his father and mother and shall be joined unto his wife and they shall become ONE FLESH. . . ."***

How clearly does our Master teach us that marriage is based on sex and bodies. With bodies belonging to the earth, marriage does too. Becoming ONE FLESH is very much an earthly matter. In fact, **everything fleshly** belongs to this life alone. The Apostle Paul was well aware of this. That's what prompted him to say, "Forget about marriage,"

> **". . . It would be better for you to continue to live as I do. But if you cannot restrain your desires, go on and marry — for it is better to marry than burn with passion."***

*Matthew 19:5   *1 Corinthians 7:8-9 T.E.V.

17

Would Paul dare to say such a thing if he really believed marriage an eternal matter? Hardly. It was because he was familiar with the **eternal plan** and knew the **temporary role** of marriage that he dared such a statement. Just how daring his words are can be seen when you recall God said, "It is not good for man to be alone." Paul seemingly contradicts God's statement when he says, "It is better not to marry."

Did the Apostle see something we didn't? You know he did. His "third heaven" experience exposed him to the realities of the next life. He knew that earthly marriages do not continue after death; that our future family has no connection with earthly family relationships. Paul's vantage point let him weigh that which was temporary against that which was eternal. His instructions are based on what he saw. And what was that, precisely? That earthly marriages and the families issuing from them are due to people becoming ONE FLESH. Whereas heaven's family is based on people becoming ONE SPIRIT. Flesh and Spirit are two different worlds.

TWO DIFFERENT WORLDS?

 It is an urgent New Testament truth that the physical world and the spirit-world are entirely different modes of existence. Once we depart this life, bodies are useless. They can't go where we're going. To suggest that bodies could be in heaven is a contradiction in terms. It's like saying darkness and light can exist together. This is why our Lord insisted:

"That which is born of the flesh is flesh: but that which is born of the Spirit is spirit" (John 3:6).

For a man to behold the Father, he must leave the physical realm. He must put everything physical behind him to enter the spirit-world, for **"God is a Spirit."** Likewise, when God would appear in the world, He too must put on a body. That's what He did. Jesus is God in human form. The point to see is that here are two different worlds. The difference between them is IN KIND, not degree — much as we find the animal and mineral kingdoms differ in kind. God has placed us in bodies for the specific purpose of isolating us and insulating us from any direct contact with the spirit-world.

In a very real sense we're prisoners in our own bodies for the time. As long as these physical prisons have life in them, we're forced to remain behind the bars of sight and sound. To live inside a body, means further that we are limited to the functions that it performs, i.e., tasting, hearing, seeing, touching, etc. Why even our thinking is limited to the brain that comes with the body. Yes, we have minds, but they are forced to use the brain that goes with the body — **until it dies.** Once the body expires, we're released from our prisons, free to do all the things everyone else does in the spirit. Of course, that is what death is all about, the day we are let out of jail!

HEAVENLY MARRIAGE—ONE SPIRIT!

While we have said, "Marriages are not made in heaven," we note the fact that **a marriage** does occur there. But only the one, the "marriage of the Lamb." As the First Adam had his bride, so the Second or Last Adam has His bride. Just as Eve was presented to Adam, so is the church to be presented to the Lord Jesus as His bride.*

"For I am jealous of you," says Paul, "with a godly jealousy; for I have BETROTHED YOU to one husband, that to CHRIST I might present you as a pure virgin" (2 Corinthians 11:2).

Paul is speaking of that day when the church will be joined to Jesus in heaven. The Revelation calls it a wedding.

"Let us be glad and give honor to Him, for the MARRIAGE OF THE LAMB has come and His BRIDE has made herself ready."*

NOTE: For a fuller treatment of our life in "earth-suits," and our departure from them, read the author's **DEATH: GRADUATION TO GLORY.** There the exodus from the body is presented as a glorious Christian experience. The mechanics, as set forth from the Scripture, are fascinating, marvellous! One reading this book gets excited about the day he will be released from his earthly prison to join the Lord and others . . . **in the spirit!**

*Ephesians 5:27   *Revelation 19:7 NAS.

This wedding occurs in the Spirit, in the heavenlies. The bride is composed of all born-again believers, those made one by the Spirit of God. On earth, weddings join ONE MAN AND ONE WOMAN, but in the Spirit, many are made ONE as they are joined to Christ. This is why I stress the difference IN KIND. In the flesh, you can only join one man to one woman, but in the Spirit, many can be joined. See how the Word of God certifies this:

"But he that is joined unto the Lord is one spirit" (1 Cor. 6:17).

Thus there is no limit to the number who make up the Bride of Christ. "Whosoever will" may come and be joined to Jesus to participate in the heavenly wedding. No matter how many wives or husbands a person has had in his earthly life, it has nothing to do with the ONE WEDDING which takes place in heaven. All that matters is being IN CHRIST.

We're accustomed to the idea of a man leaving his father and mother to become ONE FLESH with a woman. Maybe it is hard to shift to the idea of what it means to become ONE SPIRIT with the Lord, but we must. That is the only union which really counts, for it is the ETERNAL ONE. What is more obvious than God's Plan of earthly marriage to prepare us for the everlasting marriage to Christ? Not only that, the heavenly marriage is more intimate. The new relationship with Christ and each other in heaven will surpass anything we have known on earth. We will thrill to TOTAL INTIMACY THERE, something not possible on earth.

MORE INTIMATE?

Absolutely. Intimacy is something we cannot fully achieve on earth. Why? We're separated from each other by bodies. There's no way to get truly close to anyone with our souls insulated by bodies. Each person is an island now, and there is no way to get to him. He's enveloped in flesh. And the flesh separates us.

Pick up your child. Squeeze him to your chest. Have you ever thought to yourself as you looked down at the darling, **"I could just eat you up!"** And what did you mean by that? **"I wish I could get closer. I wish I could somehow digest**

your being with my own." I suppose that sounds awkward. You must sense what I am saying. We yearn to be spirit-to-spirit with people, but we can't as long as these bodies isolate us. The closest we can come now, is **body-to-body.** The sex-privilege is of the same order. It is body — yet never **total** intimacy.

Marriage brings the lovely privilege of sexual satisfaction. Two people can give sweet fulfillment to each other — but it's not enough, not nearly enough. Besides, it is so temporary. Not long after one sex experience is memory, the hunger returns. It is impossible for people to be REALLY CLOSE as long as bodies separate our souls.

Can I tell you what true, spiritual intimacy is really like? No. I don't know. But surely the sex-privilege is a clue. If the satisfaction of our bodies can be so pleasurable and thrilling, what must be the satisfaction of our souls? When God installed the sex-experience, He meant it to be terrific! He wants man to delight in the marriage-bed. Yet for all its consuming pleasure it cannot meet the deepest longings of the soul and its yearning for intimacy. Multiplied sex-experiences may answer the repeated cries of the body, but sex cannot satisfy the soul.

Man was designed for intimacy with God . . . and that, **in the Spirit.** Hence there is only one way to become intimate with Him . . . **spiritual union with Jesus Christ!** This spiritual union is to our souls, what the physical sex union is to our bodies. Referring to those who are truly joined to the Lord Jesus, it is written:

"And you are complete in Him!"*

This is the completeness, the thrilling intimacy for which our souls yearn. If we think the sex-privilege is marvellous, what must it be like eternally joined to the One WHO designed the sex-experience in the first place! If He could provide something so wonderful for our bodies, what must be in store for our souls! Of course, it is impossible to picture the completeness which will be ours when we are at last rid of the flesh. I know now the tender thrill of my own dear

---

*Colossians 2:10a

wife. But surely it is miserable by comparison with what God has in store for those who love Jesus!*

WHAT DOES THIS DO TO EARTHLY MARRIAGE?

Should the fact that human marriage is earthly and temporary in any way hinder its part in God's plan? No. It's purpose remains clearly that of getting us ready to live with ONE PERSON — Christ Jesus! This is why the Word insists on one woman and one man joined for life. Don't you think it ingenious that a man and woman could become **one flesh** during their earthly lives in anticipation of becoming ONE SPIRIT with Christ throughout eternity?

Far from weakening the role of marriage, it enhances it. It is no small matter to be joined to one person and **"cleave only unto him as long as ye both shall live."** It is the doing of just that which prepares us to give ourselves totally to the Lord.

Here's what happens to marriage.

It makes it an earthly drama, a play. When God assigns you a body, which He does at birth (for your parents have no control over your being a boy or girl), your role in the drama is determined. If you receive a male body, you will play the part of Christ. If your body is female, you will play the part of the church. Then, at some point in your social history you join your sexual opposite to act out the truth of Christ and His church. Naturally, all of it is preparatory to the great wedding scheduled to occur in heaven — the marriage of the Lamb. For the time you are merely **acting.** In heaven, it will be the real thing.

That's what marriage is, role playing. And your body determines your part.

Why a chapter on this? The truth that marriage is a TEMPORARY ARRANGEMENT can ease many unnecessary heartaches suffered by Christians. When you can see clearly just how temporary your present marriage arrangement is, and that it is but a play, you will look upon it differently:

---

*1 Corinthians 2:9

1.   You can deal differently with a person when you know he is NOT going to be your husband in the next life.

2.   It can drastically affect the way a wife dwells with an unsaved mate.

3.   Who minds parting with an unsaved husband when you know that all such relationships terminate at death and have no meaning in the life to come.

4.   If you are single and one who never marries, it is comforting to understand you are not forfeiting an eternal companion.

5.   If you come to Christ, but your marriage partner refuses, this in no way interferes with your carrying out your role. You can still play your part and get ready for the future marriage.

6.   Perhaps you are one of those who have erringly (or innocently) married the "wrong man." It is a relief to know that God can make **any man** the "right man." It disposes of the notion that there is a "certain man" for every woman. This is not to say that God sanctions the knowing choice of an unsaved husband. Indeed not. He forbids it. To deliberately YOKE oneself to an unbeliever violates the drama. Paul speaks strongly against this, (2 Corinthians 6:14). But where it has occurred **inadvertantly,** a knowledge of the temporary nature of marriage can keep a partner from despair. It also cancels Satan's power to produce guilt feelings i.e., "Now you've done it. You've ruined your life." Very often the opposite is true and God accomplishes His will more perfectly in such a situation. Romans 8:28 applies here, too.

7.   Where one is the victim in a divorce, it removes the haunting notion that an eternal bond has been dissolved. Inasmuch as marriage pictures our eternal union with Jesus, divorce is not a part of God's plan. The Word says, God hates divorce (Mal. 2:16). But it does happen. And when it does, the victim finds great relief knowing the temporary nature of earthly marriage.

NOTE: Comforting insight for casualties of the marriage program is offered in the author's book, **THE COMPASSIONATE SIDE OF DIVORCE.**

WHEN GOD TAKES MARJORIE

 For over 32 years Margie and I have been joyously wedded. We were saved together, we now serve together, and our lives are as full and complete as they can be. Like others in love, we have become so close it is frequently unnecessary for us to speak. A look passes the message between us. We anticipate each other's thoughts. It's fun to be together, a sad emptiness to be apart. It's impossible for me to think of life with anyone else.

And yet — I am glad she will **not** be my wife in heaven. Shocked? Our relationship will be even better there. Two glorious words . . . "IN CHRIST," guarantee a new and different **intimacy** for us, one which will exceed anything we have known in this world. We will not only be intimate with Jesus and each other, but also every other born-again child of God.

It delights me to think that one day I will BE CLOSER to Margie than I am now. I am ready to let go of our earthly marriage knowing God will replace it with an even deeper bond in Christ. A day is coming for Margie and me . . . yes, for you too, when we will be closer to each other than anything we have dreamed in this life.

"Closer than breathing, nearer than hands or feet . . ." is the way someone put it.

As precious as my earthly marriage is, I will gladly trade it for what awaits when the "marriage of the Lamb is come!" God has never taken anything from me that He didn't replace it with something better. Surely marriage will be no exception. I anticipate joys exceeding my most cherished moments with Margie. I can tell you there have been times with her when my spirit has soared to the heavenlies. As marvellous as it all has been, living with Jesus and you will be even better.

COMFORT

If you are one who has said goodbye to a Christian mate, you may draw deep comfort from these words. Your relationship with your partner will surpass anything you enjoyed in this life.

If you are one who is suffering under the agony of an unequal yoke, you can look forward to the day when it will be lifted — permanently. If your husband dies outside of Christ, it will have no effect on your future joy or soul's satisfaction in the Lord.

More important, though, is that wife who wants to be God's servant toward her husband. Who yearns to see him saved and is willing to do what she must to bring him to Christ. She is the one for whom this book was written. Many live for Jesus inside miserable and difficult marriages. Can we ease the squeeze?

Not close enough

Chapter Three

THE SHOW MUST GO ON!

Governor Reagan recalls a humorous incident which occurred while he hosted the General Electric Theater. During a "live" telecast a famous actor momentarily forgot his lines. He had to improvise a cover up. Ingeniously he began to move his lips as though speaking, yet he uttered no sounds. The listeners, hearing no words, thought the sound had gone off their sets. Some reached for the knobs for better tuning. As soon as the actor recovered his lines, he spoke aloud. The viewing public was none the wiser.

Actors learn to improvise. They become skilled in meeting the unpredictable which often occurs during live drama. It is unthinkable that the show would be stopped or that an actor would walk off the stage. It has become tradition in the theater that no matter what happens . . . **"The show must go on!"**

MARRIAGE—A LIVE DRAMA

Since marriage is also a drama the same tradition applies. Marriage is a "live" play, the most serious drama of life. As soon as a man and woman say "I do," the curtain rises. Those words, "So long as ye both shall live," mean the show must go on . . . **no matter what!** Since it is a live show, the actors are not to walk off because trouble develops. Instead, they are expected to adjust, improvise and meet situations with ingenuity. There's no provision for walking off stage written into the script. A Script? Yes, there's one.

 Startling to think of marriage as a play? Then likely you are meeting for the first time that it is just that—AND NOTHING MORE. As with any play, this one also has its Producer, Author, Director and a Script which calls for the different roles and has a basic plot. Furthermore, there are costumes, actors and a stage on which to perform. Just about everything you know

about the theater can be applied to marriage, once you understand that it is a play.

Let's see how your knowledge of dramatic productions can help to understand God's design in marriage.

The Producer of the Drama

God has employed drama as a teaching device ever since He began revealing His purposes to man. You are familiar, of course, with His big production of Old Testament times. He took an entire nation and for 1400 years had the people act out the truth of Christ's coming as the sin-bearer. They slaughtered animals, sprinkled blood, transported a tabernacle and performed priestly rituals. All this to dramatize on the stage of the world, the truth of . . . **"The Lamb of God which taketh away the sin of the world!"** (John 1:29).

Those with spiritual vision were able to watch the play and behold the redemption scheme. Naturally it was symbolical. It could only shadow the real truth. When Jesus came the drama ended. Its work was finished. There was no longer a need for symbols when the Sacrificial Lamb arrived in the world to . . . **"put away sin by the sacrifice of Himself"** (Heb. 9:26).

That Old Testament show was a smash. It ran for 1400 years, a long run for any play. The world watched a cast of more than 3 million people dramatize the redemption story year after year. It was wonderful, beautifully accurate. The fact that the world didn't want God's Lamb doesn't mean the play was a flop. It did its job. What Sunday School teacher hasn't taught the thrilling description of Christ's ministries in the tabernacle! Its message was clear enough. In fact, God made sure Moses set it up . . . exactly as it was given to him in the mount.* He followed the Script to the letter.

Today God is using another drama.

Again the stage is the world. Those with spiritual vision can see how **Christian** marriage dramatizes the truth of Christ and His church. That is the revelation God would now make by means of the marriage drama. The action

---

*Exodus 25:40

27

pictures the intimacy between the believer and his Lord. Apparently not too many understood the 1400 year drama of Israel. We might well wonder how many understand the significance of Christian marriage today. But that it is definitely a drama . . . and that it pictures Christ and His church . . . is clearly stated by the Apostle:

"For this cause shall a man leave his father and mother and shall be joined to his wife and the two shall become one flesh. This is a great MYSTERY, but I speak CONCERNING CHRIST and HIS CHURCH!" (Eph. 5:31, 32).

Ever ponder those verses? Sure you do. God isn't hiding anything here. He's revealing it! And to those with eyes to see. As with Israel, the drama of Christian marriage will also one day end. In a coming hour, Christian marriage will be replaced by the real thing — "the marriage of the lamb!" What further use will there be for the symbolical, shadowy enactment of our relationship to Jesus when we are finally with Him — face to face! Dear reader, may God anoint your eyes to see the real majesty of marriage: the drama of Christ and His church.

PLAYERS WEAR COSTUMES

In any play you recognize the role by the player's costume. But what is the costume in marriage? **Our bodies.** The body a person receives from the Lord determines the part he or she is to play in the drama whether MALE or FEMALE. You recall we have already referred to the human body as an "earth-suit" for the invisible image of God. Now we can describe it more specifically. It is a COSTUME. It dresses the person inside in either male or female garb.

The one wearing the male body is handed the HUSBAND script. The person in female dress receives the WIFE script. The play is under way as soon as the couple exchanges vows. From there on the script is to be followed to the letter. Again let me remind you that the husband and wife roles are merely parts in the marriage play. Each player's role lasts only so long as he wears his costume. When the costume is shed at death, he is no longer on stage. The play is over as far as he or she is concerned.

"I DO."

The preacher says, **"I now pronounce you man and wife,"** and the play opens. From that moment the players forsake their personal freedoms and dedicate themselves to performing their parts. They step into their roles. The trip to the altar ends freedom to live as one pleases. Once a man and a woman undertake to act out the truth of Christ and His church, they are to perform with all the resourcefulness they can — no matter what comes along. Nothing short of tragedy is to interfere.

Next, the plot. What an ingenious scheme it is.

THE PLOT OF THE DRAMA

The plot is actually a pot — a pressure pot!

As a boy I took curious interest in Grandma's pressure cooker. It was a large kettle with huge screws all around the top which clamped the lip down tightly. A gage was mounted in the lid. You could read the dial as the pressure rose inside. It told how much fire to put under the pot. There was a safety valve to prevent an explosion.

You know about pressure cookers? Modern ones are quite different from Grandma's, but they do the same thing. The heat and pressures combine to break down the fibre in the vegetables and tenderize the toughest meats. The cheaper roasts yield under pressure. Pressure cookers are great for turning tough foods into delicious dinners and — **sinners into saints!**

When God says, "Till death do you part," He is clamping the lid on marriage. He knows the pressures will build, He counts on it. He expects these pressures to break down our stubborn resistance to change. He knows they are necessary for reshaping our personalities. In time, when the stresses of marriage have done their work, we begin to look more and more like Jesus. That is what is supposed to take place as we polish our roles.

No pressure—no change.

Ever listen to people claiming a perfect marriage? They boast they have no arguments, insisting that romance prevails year in and year out. Take another look. What do you see. People who are NOT CHANGING. Why should they? They like things the way they are. God hates that. He despises the status quo. He wants change and that's the whole point of the plot. That's why it's a pot. The marriage program is God's chief means for producing His likeness in us.

● Marriage without pain or pressure is contrary to the divine intention. This is not to say there are no delights and joy in Christian marriage. Indeed there are. The real blessedness is exceeded only by heaven itself. But such matters are beyond the scope of this book. This is not a plan for getting the most out of your marriage. We are dealing specifically with the problem of living with an unsaved husband. A key word you will meet later in the book is . . . "Pressure." I am introducing you to it now, so that you will know that pressure is a part of our technique for dealing with an unsaved mate.

It bears repeating that this whole life is one of stress. If marriage is at the center of life as we know it, then marriage is itself the **center of stress.** I didn't say distress. I said stress. As the pressure cooker applies stress to its contents, marriage applies stress to the partners. And there is a safety valve on the pressure-pot. God guarantees not to stress the Christian actor with more than he can bear:

> **"No temptation has overtaken you but such as is common to man; and God is faithful, who will not allow you to be tempted beyond what ye are able; but with the temptation will provide a way of escape, that you may be able to endure it."***

That's the safety valve. Later, we'll see how it works.

THE PLAYERS STUDY THEIR SCRIPTS

The top of the Script is marked **WIFE'S PART.** The Holy Script Writer is specific!

---

*1 Corinthians 10:13

"Wives submit yourselves unto your own husbands as unto the Lord!"*

The person wearing the FEMALE costume receives her script from the Director, the Holy Spirit. She studies it, then asks:

Wife: "You mean you want me to pretend the MALE lead is the boss?"

Director: "You can think of it like that, but it's not really as though you were an employee working for a boss. It's more like your own body as it receives instructions from your head. I want you to look upon your husband as part of yourself. Put it like this . . . he thinks and you act."

Wife: "I see. But how far do I carry this?"

Director: "Now don't get upset. Remember you are acting out the truth of Christ and the church, therefore . . . 'as the church is subject to Christ, so also the wives ought to be subject to their husbands in everything!' " (Eph. 5:24 NAS.)

Wife: "That could be a little hard under certain circumstances, couldn't it? That 'all things' might get a little sticky if carried to extreme?"

Director: "I'm aware of that, but don't worry. That's what I am here for. I'll help you with your part. After you get used to my coaching, you'll find it's not so bad. Besides, anything gets easier after you do it a few times."

Wife: "All right. I'll try. But I know right now you'll have to help me. There are bound to be situations which are beyond me, so if you see me looking in your direction, you'll know I need help."

Director: "I will, that's a promise."

Wife: "What if the male lead asks me to do something I just don't want to do? What then?"

Director: "The Script calls for you to submit, so you'll have to forget what you do or don't want to do. Do it anyway, for my sake. Yet it is important that you perform your part as written. So you will do it for Me, won't you?"

---
*Ephesians 5:22

31

Wife: "But suppose we simply can't get along? What if there are serious dis-
agreements and I can't stand the guy?"

Director: "Come on, be a good trooper. You don't have to like the star. Put
yourself into the part. I know all about those feelings, but the play
is ruined unless you follow the Script."

Wife: "You coach me and I'll give my best to the part."

Director: "Good for you. Now you in the MALE costume, Mr. Husband. Come
here for a minute? I want to go over your part with you."

The Husband's part.

If the wife's script is specific, the husband's is detailed.

"Husbands love your wives, just as Christ loved the church and
gave Himself up for her; that He might sanctify her, having
cleansed her by the washing of the water of the Word, that He
might present to Himself a church in all her glory, having no spot
or wrinkle or any such thing; but that she might be holy and
blameless. Husbands ought also to love their wives as their
own bodies. He who loves his wife loves himself; for no one
ever hated his own flesh, but nourishes and cherishes it, just as
Christ also does the church, because we are His body" (Eph.
5:25-29).

Director: "Now you are the star. That means the responsibility for the success
of the show rests on you. If you let down, the play is ruined."

Husband: "You mean the show is built around me?"

Director: "That's right. Now let's go over your role.
You represent Christ in the story. You are to demonstrate His love
and care for His church by the way you cherish your wife and provide
for her. That part is played by the lady over there. Though you
represent the Lord, that doesn't mean that you are the head of the
house. In fact you're not. You are the head of the wife only. That
means she is to you what your own body is. You are to treat her
as you would the most delicate part of your own body. Ever hear
of a man hating his own eyes or lungs, for example."

Husband: "No."

Director: "That's not all. Since she submits to you, you are responsible for what she becomes as she lives with you. Jesus went the limit in providing for His church, you are to sacrifice yourself in providing a wondrous marriage climate where your wife can blossom into her radiant best. As the Lord Jesus is now preparing His bride, so should your sacrificial love bring that lady over there to perfection. That is a long way from your being a self-indulgent lord of the manor. Do you understand?"

Husband: "I think so. You mean, because she voluntarily dethrones her will to make me her lord, I am responsible for what she becomes as the result of our marriage."

Director: "Right. I have designed her so that her glory comes through making you complete. You see we can't have two stars, two leaders in the marriage. So one is designed to give the leadership, and the other to follow. It will be all right, because I have designed each with the right emotional qualities to play these parts. Now if you carry off your role as it's written there, we'll have a lovely play and the audience will see exactly how it is with Christ and His church."

Husband: "Okay. But I must be honest. I always thought my part was the head of the house. I didn't realize my real job was preparing my wife for the marriage of the Lamb. Now that I understand, I'll see what I can do about cultivating her with love and affection and providing a home that allows her to blossom into a beautiful Christian woman.

Director: "That's the stuff. I think we have the roles clear now. Let's go to work on the parts and get familiar with them."

ON WITH THE SHOW

"Hey! Stop the show! We can't go on. My husband isn't a Christian!"

Oh, the male star is not a Christian? Too bad. But we must continue. You signed a contract, you married him. The roles are established and opening night is behind us. We can't cancel just because your husband is not a Christian.

"But should we go on? Our marriage isn't picturing Christ and the church?"

We can't stop because the MALE star isn't what we need in the part. It only means you'll have to perform your role that much better. You will be carrying the show. People will be watching you. At least the production will feature half the story, the church's loving submission to Christ.

> **"You mean, even though the MALE star isn't a Christian, I should carry out the role of the church anyway? I don't see how I can submit myself as I should to an unsaved man!"**

Ah, ah, ah . . . remember, you're not submitting to him alone. I am the Director. Do it for Me. Keep your eyes on Me. Did I not tell you when I assigned you your part that it should be played . . . "as unto the Lord?" So you will give it your best, won't you? To encourage you, I'll say this . . . THE BETTER YOU PLAY YOUR PART, THE MORE LIKELY YOUR HUSBAND WILL BE SAVED!"

SAVED?

> **"For the unbelieving husband is sanctified through his wife . . ."**
> (1 Cor. 7:14a).

Read that before? Sure you have. Pondered its significance? It makes a Christian wife who is married to an unsaved man . . . a **special agent for God!** The heathen husband living with a Christian woman is marked for special treatment. He is set apart, separated from other men and chained by marriage to a child of God. That means, he is sharing his earthly life with a person who is in position to offer eternal life to him.

You see, the word "Sanctified," does not always mean, **saved,** neither does it always mean, **cleansed.** There is another meaning . . . **"Separated and set apart."** Recall that the vessels and even the tabernacle itself were sanctified? Our modern word, "Sanctuary," means a building set apart for a specific purpose unto the Lord. This is the sense in which it is used in the verse above. The unsaved husband is separated from the masses of men and marked for **special treatment** by the Lord.

It is no small thing for an unbeliever to be yoked to a believer . . . 365 days a year. Where can he run? There's no place to flee without abandoning his home and family. Thus he is different from any other prospect. He is a special case . . . remarkably set apart for Gospel treatment. His wife is God's special agent to keep the Gospel challenge before him continually.

Special Agent

Did you know that you are God's special agent, commissioned to reach your unsaved husband? Christian wife, you are surely God's chosen servant to deal with him. No one can reach that man more powerfully than you. Don't think to shrug off this responsibility by asking the pastor to come by, or wait for some soul-winner to cross his path and lead him to Jesus. You're God's agent. You are as fully set apart for the task as your husband is set apart for the treatment.

And don't think to PRAY him into the kingdom either.

> **"What are you saying! I thought it was God's promise that we who trust in the Lord could count on Him to save our families. After all, doesn't the Bible say . . . 'Believe on the Lord Jesus Christ and thou shalt be saved AND THY HOUSE.'"***

You bet it says that. But that isn't all it says. Read the next verse:

> **"And they spake unto him the Word of the Lord and to ALL THAT WERE IN HIS HOUSE."**

See that? Did you ever hear of anyone being saved apart from hearing the Word of God? No. You know that "faith cometh by hearing, and hearing by the Word of God."* It's inescapable. There is no way to circumvent the ministry of God's Word. People cannot believe in Whom they have not heard and they cannot be saved apart from believing in Him. Now look at verse 34 of that same chapter and see what really did happen in the jailor's house . . .

---

*Acts 16:31   *Romans 10:17

35

> **"And when he brought them into his house, he set meat before them, and rejoiced, believing in God WITH ALL HIS HOUSE!"**

There! His house believed too! The members of the jailor's household heard the Word of God and believed it. That's how they were saved. Not because Paul promised blanket salvation to the jailor's family if he would but turn to Christ. So let's not hear any talk of your trusting God for the **automatic salvation** of your husband, because you are a believer. That just can't happen.

What is true, is that you are God's agent with a job to do. It cannot be side-stepped by taking a verse out of context, hoping to blackmail God with it. No, No. I'm not bawling you out. I know that it is popular to shake this verse in God's face at prayer meeting. I do want to startle you enough so that you will take a hard look at the wonderful privilege God has set before you. It is exciting to be an agent of the Most High. And you will thrill to some of that excitement as you read the next chapter. You will like dealing with your husband . . . WHEN YOU KNOW HOW. That's the point of this book.

WHEN THE CURTAIN COMES DOWN

This chapter has featured earthly marriage as a play. Unique, ingenious, but still a play. Oh, the wisdom that designed the earthly rehearsal for the heavenly wedding! But, as with all plays, this lovely drama also ends. There comes a time when you cease your ACTING to participate in the real experience with the Lord Jesus.

And when is that? The instant death strikes your body. In that second you are relieved of your part. But not until then. This is why . . . "till death do us part," is a part of the vow. Death is the final scene for you. Then you slip out of your costume. No longer is your personality clothed in a MALE or FEMALE garment for the show is over. You are yourself from then on, no longer an actress.

● When Jesus came the Old Testament drama ended. There was no point in portraying the truth of the Sin-bearer after Jesus arrived and took away sin. There is no need for continuing with rehearsals after the wedding has taken place. Once you enter into the eternal fellowship with Christ, all preparation for it ends.

But until that day, you give your best as an actress. You polish your part, letting the stresses of marriage refine your personality. . . . You learn to devote yourself to your mate no matter how rough it gets. Your mind dwells on the day when you will live only for Jesus. You think to yourself . . .

"If I can live with this man on earth and survive the crises of marriage, how much more wonderful will it be living with Christ who loves me enough to die for me!"

You don't mind getting ready for eternity, even if you have to live with an unsaved man. Such a thing can be an adventure in the Spirit if you have a plan. Don't you find it fascinating to consider that you are God's agent, set apart to bring His special working to a lost soul? That's intriguing. The fascination mounts when you consider this man is your husband, joined to you for life.

You bet it is fascinating. It's thrilling. And the more so when you have a definite plan for working with the Holy Spirit. Wouldn't you like to be able to squeeze your husband's soul . . . **in the power of God!**

We come to that now.

Chapter Four

THE NUTCRACKER TECHNIQUE

Take a walnut. Now pick up the nutcracker. Insert the walnut and squeeze **"Cracccck!"** That's the way to deal with an unsaved husband. Put him in the nutcracker and squeeze. Something has to give — one way or the other. This chapter is about — the NUTCRACKER TECHNIQUE. It introduces you to a specific plan for dealing with your unsaved husband. Picture yourself as maneuvering that man between the jaws of a huge nutcracker and . . . **squeezing!**

Where did the idea come from? It's not mine. Something the Lord Jesus said gave birth to this exciting concept:

> **"Let your light so shine before men that they may see your good works and glorify your Father which is in heaven"** (Matt. 5:16).

Naturally you're familiar with that verse. But you are wondering, **"What does it have to do with a nutcracker? And how does Brother Lovett hope to connect it with unsaved husbands?"** You'll see. Once you behold how it works, I'm sure you'll acknowledge the plan is of the Lord. Not only does it do a great job on your husband, but it glorifies the Lord Jesus Christ in a startling way.

A NUTCRACKER?

Almost everyone has used one at some time or another. It's simple to position a nut in place and bear down on the jaws. There is so much leverage the shell has to yield. Our nutcracker has two jaws too. They are indicated in the verse above. See those two words: LIGHT and WORKS? Those are the jaws. Visualize a giant nutcracker. One handle is marked . . . LIGHT, the other is labeled . . . WORKS. The Holy Spirit joins the two together so that you can bear down on those handles and get all the squeeze you want. The nut in the middle is your unsaved husband. Apply enough pressure and his resistance shell has to crack.

LIGHT
WORKS

Maybe it has never struck you that a Christian's LIGHT and his WORKS are two different things. They are not the same at all, though you often hear Christians equating them. Not infrequently does someone say, "I believe in letting my light shine." And what does he mean? Usually, that he tries to live a good life before others. But a good life has to do with **works,** not LIGHT. Let me tell you what happened to me one night. It was God's unique way of dramatizing the startling difference between LIGHT and WORKS.

It was late and I was driving a lonely stretch of road. My car began to sputter. Somehow the Lord kept it going until I came within sight of an all-night gas station. Then it quit. A mechanic was on duty. He came with his helper to take a look. Together they searched under the hood for the trouble. Then he announced, **"Your fuel pump is out, but we can install another in a jiffy."**

He sent his helper back to the station. Shortly he returned with the new pump. I. waited while they worked. The mechanic had his head buried under the hood, while his helper held a flashlight. Somehow the lad let his attention wander. The light shifted. The mechanic exploded . . .

"Hey! What do you think I have you here for? Shine that light on my work so I can see what I am doing!"

The Spirit nudged. My mind went instantly to Jesus' Word, "Let your light so shine that men can see your good works." Ah, ha. He was teaching me a lesson. Dramatically I was observing the difference between LIGHT and WORKS. Of course, they weren't the same thing. That mechanic's work was one thing, but the light was something else. Without it, neither he nor those watching could see what he was doing. The light was necessary to **illuminate** the work so it could **be seen.**

So they are different. This is why one jaw is definitely made up of the Christian's LIGHT. We'll get to the other jaw in a bit. First we need to see what constitutes the Christian's light. Just what is it? What does Jesus mean when He says, "Let your light shine?"

LIGHT

We know about light. Most of us have stubbed our toe in the dark while groping for the switch. Then . . . "Click!" Ah, those comforting rays which reveal everything around us. They let us see what we're doing and where we're going. Yes, we know how light from the sun, a bulb or a flame can illuminate things about us.

But there's another kind of illumination. And we're familiar with it too. It's the kind meant by the common expression, **"Shed light on the subject."** By that we mean **information, intelligence** or **knowledge** which opens up or explains an otherwise unrevealed matter. We know what the corresponding darkness is too. It is ignorance. When an obscure subject is illuminated by information we say we have light on the subject. When that happens a person often says, "Oh, I see." That means he has just acquired **insight.** Physical light exposes things outside, information explains things inside. That's why we call it **insight.**

It is in this sense that the Lord Jesus uses the word "light." Just as sunlight scatters the darkness of the night, so does God's Word dispel the inner or spiritual darkness of this world. Without the WORD OF GOD, men have no idea as to who they are, where they are from or where they are going. Until life is viewed under the Holy Light of God's Word, people cannot understand themselves or the world in which they live. Nothing makes sense, for it can't be seen as it is. What am I really saying?

God's Word is His Light!

The Psalmist said the same thing:

"The entrance of thy words giveth light."*

and again,

"Thy word is a Lamp unto my feet and a light unto my path."**

There. God's Word shines. It's like a street light scattering the spiritual darkness of this world. And those who use or declare God's Word are illuminators. They are informers who bring insight to people so they can **see** what God is doing in their lives. They are like helpers holding the flashlight, so that God's WORK can be seen. Now if God's Word is His Light, what is "your light" that is to shine?

Your Light.

If God's Light is His Word, then your light is YOUR WORD. As surely as God's Word shines on His works to illuminate them, so can your light shine on your works. And what will men see? God's hand in your life. Without this light they will not see what God is doing, no matter how startling or dramatic it may be. No matter how spectacular the working of God is in your life, men will neither see it nor credit God for it.

 Take the sun for example. Here is an amazing thing God provides. It rises each morning to fill the sky with its glory. There is no place a person can go

*Psalm 119:130   **Psalm 119:105

41

to escape its witness. But do men wonder about it? Do they ask how it happens to maintain its schedule? Does it occur to them how such a thing could not organize itself into a light-giving program? No. If men can behold such a dazzling wonder in the sky and fail to see God's hand, surely they will never credit Him for a small wonder in your life — UNLESS YOU SAY SO.

IT'S LIKE THIS

Perhaps you may recall this story from "Witnessing Made Easy."

I once had a dear friend whose wife was hospitalized with polio. For eight years she lay in an iron lung until God released her from that prison of flesh. Faithfully, three times a week, year in and year out, my brother would visit her. People saw his faithfulness and said, **"Oh, isn't he a good man!"** Beyond that, he did a great job caring for the children by himself. He gave them discipline and Christian training. People also saw this and said, **"Oh, isn't he a wonderful father?"**

His language was pure. He refused to speak evil against anyone. He was faithful in serving his church. Again they noted, **"What a fine man he is."** Of course, he was a fine man. He truly loved the Lord and endured hardship because the Lord stood by him. But the people saw only my friend and his devotion to his family and church. They didn't once consider that it was Jesus who made it possible. They merely thought, **"What a wonderful person. I could never do that!"**

You tell me who got the credit, who got the praise? The people saw his good works but who did they glorify? They marvelled at my brother, but they did not glorify his Father which was in heaven. Why not? **His light was not shining.** There were no **words** to illuminate the precious working of God in his life. Nothing from him indicated the Lord was responsible. Until he opened his mouth to credit the Lord specifically, no one was about to acknowledge the goodness of our Master.

● Then we talked about it. At once he saw the difference between his WORKS and his LIGHT. He began to open his mouth. After that everyone who commented on his good works learned from him that it was Jesus Who made it all possible. He gave the Lord full credit for everything. Then a new stream of comment arose . . .

> "If the Lord can do that for Mr. .... maybe He can do it for me."

People were forced to behold the grace of the Lord Jesus, because of the WORD of this man. His words illuminated his works compelling people to credit Christ for them, whether they wanted to or not. Without his words, he alone got the glory. So it is not merely an interesting Bible observation we're making here. It is vital and critical that we separate our LIGHT from our WORKS. When we do this properly, we have a marvelous tool for exalting Christ—and dealing with your unsaved husband.

NOW FOR THE WORKS.

The other jaw of the nutcracker is labeled, WORKS. Can't use a nutcracker with only one jaw. It takes LIGHT and WORKS to provide the squeeze. In Chapter Three we described the wife's role in the marriage drama. She SUBMITS. Submitting to her husband and living so as to PLEASE HIM is her part in the play. Yet, she does not do this for the husband's sake alone. She does her part **"as unto the Lord."** She performs with one eye on the Director. As the Director leads and coaches, her life CHANGES.

Now that's a magic word, **change.** Recall that God is bringing us to maturity. That's what this life is about. With marriage at the center of life, it becomes God's chief lab for bringing us to maturity. **Who can mature without changing?** No one. Maturity means change. As soon as a CHANGE occurs, a wife has a definite WORK on which to shine her light.

Change you see, has a magic of its own. I won't forget the affect it had on one marriage where I was privileged to serve as counselor.

43

Long before we had heard of such a thing as the "Nutcracker Technique," a lady came to see me. She was desperate, at the end of her rope. She was begging for help with an alcoholic husband. I could see she meant it. She said she had reached her limit in suffering abuse and humiliation and poverty as the result of his drinking. When I asked what she had done so far in her attempts to dissuade him, she replied:

> "Well, I've begged that man, argued with him and preached at him for years. I've threatened to leave him, quoted the Bible countless times and God only knows how hard I've prayed for him. But nothing seems to work. I don't see anything else to try. I think we'll have to call it quits!"

> **"I see. But it does occur to me there's one thing you have not tried as yet."**

> "What's that?"

> **"Have you seriously prayed for changes in yourself instead of your husband? That is, have you asked God to make the necessary changes in you which could salvage your husband and then gone to work on those things you felt could be improved?"**

> "No. But I've tried everything else. If you think it would help. I'm willing to do that."

She did. And the results were startling. Her husband never got drunk again. He didn't have to. One of her very first changes removed the cause of his drinking. In this case it was the MAGIC of change in the wife that brought about the MIRACLE of change in the husband.

● I have told this simply to focus on the **power of change.** It does have its own magic. Ever watch a married couple that does not go out together often. But when they do, how differently they behave? Around the house and in the middle of their routine they are plain old married folk. But all dressed up and out for a good time together, they kiss, hold hands and behave quite differently. Why? This interruption in their marriage routine provides a change. It is axiomatic that **change produces change.**

THE NUTCRACKER

Now we can see God's wisdom in the nutcracker technique. While those two jaws are called LIGHT and WORKS, we see now what they really mean. A wife's WORKS are those changes in her life which take place as she looks to the Holy Spirit for direction. The changes are such that they bring PLEASURE to the husband. She lives to please him, yet doing so as **coached by the Director.** One jaw of the nutcracker therefore employs the magic of change.

The other jaw, LIGHT, is clearer too. The wife's light is her word which credits the Lord Jesus for the change in her life. She opens her mouth to illuminate her works in such a way that her husband can **see** that they are due to the Lord's presence in her life. Her words carefully point out that Christ is the One responsible for the changes. Thus he is compelled to take note of Christ.

OBSERVE: This is not preaching. She is not giving her husband God's Word, but her own. This is her own light, the very one Jesus said was to shine. She is explaining that the changes in her life are due to her desire to please both her husband and her Lord. She is not reciting Scripture passages (God's Light), neither is she asking her husband for any response. All she is doing is illuminating her works so that he can see their real source. That's all. And that is what LIGHT is supposed to do . . . illuminate.

You can see what is happening. A man suddenly finds that the Lord he has ignored, is now **at work in his own home!** And it is something he must now live with. Lovely changes take place in his wife, changes which please him greatly, but no sooner does he notice them, than he finds he must credit the Lord Jesus for them. As his home gets sweeter, he becomes more indebted to Christ. Living with this day in and day out brings terrific pressure to bear on him. Obviously, the more changes, the more light. That's what brings the greater squeeze.

Since you have used a nutcracker, you know very well that what couldn't possibly be cracked with your fingers, is easily shattered between the jaws of a nutcracker. Tremendous pressure is exerted as you bear down on those handles. The pressure can be steadily increased until that stubborn shell crumbles.

USING THE NUTCRACKER

Would you mind if I took what you already know about using a nutcracker to further explain this technique for dealing with your unsaved husband? Some obvious principles flow from the basic idea.

1. Equal force on the jaws.

When you squeeze a nutcracker you must apply equal pressure on the handles. You do it so automatically you never stop to think about it. Yet it is true. The shell of the nut yields only because it is caught between equal pressures.

What does this mean to our technique? The force applied on both jaws should be the same. That means that the

Can't crack a nut with only one jaw!

LIGHT AND THE WORKS SHOULD MATCH. The words should not exceed the works and the works are useless without the words. In other words, a wife who is submissive, doing all she can to please her husband is wasting her time if she fails to credit Christ for the changes. Similarly, the woman who is churchy without change, has only one jaw of the nutcracker in operation. Consequently there is no squeeze. It takes equal pressure to crack the shell.

Let's consider actual cases:

Years ago a lady in my congregation was deeply concerned for her unsaved husband. She spoke continually of her desire to see him saved. She bent over backwards to please him, indulging in things distasteful to her just because he asked it. BUT . . . she was reluctant to credit the Lord for this submission of her life. She was afraid she might offend her husband by suggesting that Christ was responsible for her sweet spirit. She thought such words would drive her husband further from the Lord.

Her works were wasted. He never once thought Jesus was responsible for the tenderness of his wife. Neither did he have any sense of being confronted with Christ in his home. There was absolutely no encounter between him and the Lord, because her light was **not shining on her works.** She was pressing only one jaw of the nutcracker. And that won't crack anything. Today her husband is still unsaved. She is just as agonized about it. Sadly she is **still** pressing on the WORKS jaw of the nutcracker only. Unless she reads this book she will most likely be doing it years from now.

On the other hand consider the Christian wife who is churchy without change. She is a vigorous person, outspoken for the Lord. She doesn't miss a chance to tell her husband what Jesus means to her. She speaks of the glory that fills her soul through knowledge of sins forgiven. She sings how Christ has lifted her out of the miry clay and set her feet on the solid rock. She's religious, she goes to meeting after meeting. She makes no bones about putting Christ ahead of everyone, her husband in particular.

47

What about this lady? Is her light shining? Some light is shining, of course. But on what? That's the rub. There's really nothing besides her church-going for her to illuminate. **No works of submission.** No sweet changes as she dethrones her own will to make her husband her head. No hard work in trying to **please** him. In fact she doesn't even care about pleasing him. She couldn't care less about pleasing an unregenerate man.

This lady's aggressiveness for Christ clearly interferes with her being a wife. Her house suffers as she outlives her independence. Her husband's needs are unimportant to her. She is not about to be "submissive in all things" as the Director has instructed. Obviously she is unaware of her role in the marriage play. She insists on being the star of the show, Director or no Director.

Like the lady described above, she is also pressing on but **one jaw** of the nutcracker. That won't crack anything. Her life isn't changing, she has no WORKS jaw. Doesn't she want him saved? Indeed. How she prays for his salvation. You should hear her at church. But she'll never see it this way. One jaw won't crack his resistance. The pressure on both jaws must match!

2. Squeeze gently at first.

That's the second important principle flowing from our basic idea. Not all nuts offer the same resistance. There's no need, for example, to come crashing down on an almond. It would mash the kernel as well as the shell. Yet a brazil nut takes considerable pressure before the shell yields. Not all men are alike in their resistance to the Lord. Unsaved husbands range all the way from those who are actually cooperative and go to church to those who angrily resist every hint of the Gospel.

So you squeeze gently at first. Some husbands won't need severe pressure, others will. Dealing with an unsaved husband is really no different from any soul-winning situation. You must always meet people where they are, then gradually shift their thinking to your point of view. If you do it too suddenly, they can become alarmed, suspecting your sanity.

You can see how a husband might think his wife had "flip-ped" should she go all out and begin applying terrific pressures in sudden moves.

● Besides it is easy to get out of balance when first starting to use the technique. It takes a little doing to learn how to match your light and your works. A person needs time to get familiar with the plan so that the proper amount of light is shining on a corresponding amount of change in her life. This doesn't come overnight. It follows then that it is best to start off easily, with gentle squeezes, easing on more pressure as you become familiar with the technique.

3. Take one area at a time.

Seldom does anyone put two nuts in a nutcracker at once. It's best to take one at a time. This observation can be applied to our technique. It means we should start off making changes in ONE AREA of our lives at a time. You can see

No no—not two at a time!

what a mistake it would be to try and reshape your whole life in one grand swoop. Besides, it takes years to revamp a life. So you select a single area and work on a specific change within that area. It wouldn't do to shock your husband with drastic changes in a lot of areas. You'd be over your head in no time at all.

This is the safest route. Since you can't know what it is finally going to take to crack your husband's resistance, you avoid the risk of too much pressure, if you work with one specific change at a time. Besides, these are **permanent** changes you are making. And they accumulate. Not only are they for the benefit of your earthly mate, but you are systematically getting yourself ready for your TRUE HUSBAND, Christ. So doing one step at a time helps you to relax and see that the changes are genuine. As you go from area to area, your whole person changes into a lovely bride for the Lord.

Now there may be areas where you CANNOT submit to your husband with a free conscience. Should he demand your participation in something you know to be contrary to the will of God, you could damage yourself with blind submission. Were you to become a part of his scheme to hurt or defraud someone, it could damage your fellowship with Christ if you participated. This is why I am suggesting **selective** changes rather than **blanket changes** in your life. You pick the areas where your submission can be made as unto the Lord.

Keep your eye on the Director. He is the One Who shepherds and governs your husband-pleasing role. Never will He lead you into ungodly or Christ-dishonoring acts. The will of your husband is not to be exalted over the will of the Lord. With a "new morality" sweeping the land, who knows what an unregenerate mate might ask of his wife. If you follow this principle of working on ONE AREA AT A TIME, you can avoid those things which the Lord would surely disapprove.

● So then, you are required to submit ONLY in those matters which you can do out of a PURE heart. You would not be submissive to any demand that carried you into sex-orgies, dope usage or criminal acts. If your husband wanted you to gamble or frequent disgusting places, because he did, you would refuse. Later you will learn how to do that, and in such a way that it becomes a part of your nutcracker technique.

With your submission, "as unto the Lord," you are obviously not required to do anything that would displease the Holy Spirit. You submit ONLY in those areas where the **Lord is pleased** by your submission. His pleasure has the priority over your husband's. Hence those words speaking of the wife's submission . . . "in all things" . . . must be qualified by the phrase, "as unto the Lord." She is **not required** to do anything which she could not do . . . "heartily as unto the Lord!" After all, any good actress follows the instructions of the Director.

4.   Start away from yourself.

Obviously it is harder to correct a fault in your personality than to change something in your surroundings. So we have another valid principle for the nutcracker. Begin the plan by selecting from your household routine, rather than in yourself. It could be something as simple as rearranging the living room so that your husband can better enjoy his TV programs. He'll notice it and then you can comment. Any husband is bound to notice something done to make him more comfortable, whether it is the timing of his meals or the way you set his table.

Changes in your person will affect him most. But it is wise to wait until you have practiced with **externals,** before attempting changes **within** yourself. You can see that kneeling to take off his shoes while he relaxes before the TV is harder on you than laying out his pajamas at the foot of the bed. One is a thoughtful act, the other self-abasing. Acts of serious self-denial are better deferred until you have gotten used to the Holy Spirit's anointing for such things. Then, of course, it becomes fun to watch what HE does with your acts. It is thrilling to see His convicting power at work in your husband as you deny yourself in the Spirit. That doesn't come overnight.

● When you shift from surroundings to yourself, begin with your outward appearance. Let it have something to do with the way you look, rather than your behavior. That is, move by steps toward your own personality. The last thing you will be working on will be a character trait. You can see, for example, how much easier it is to fix your hair in the morning than hold your tongue when he says the wrong thing. Or, that getting out of that bathrobe earlier is easier than ceasing to worry when something goes wrong.

So start the plan with household changes first. Then graduate to your appearance. Finally you will be working on your personality. In all, submit yourself **to the Lord** for the task of **pleasing** your husband. No matter which area you select for change, the plan always works the same. You make a change. He observes it and comments. Then your light clicks on, something like this:

"CLICK" . . .

"I'm so glad you noticed, dear. But don't give me the credit. It wasn't until the Lord showed me the kind of wife I am supposed to be, that I even cared about doing these things. The thanks is really His, since He is the One responsible for my desire to be a good wife to you."

There—that's the general idea. As a Christian wife, you are always sweet. You live to please your husband because it is your role. You acknowledge the Lord Jesus in every change. Sound familiar? It should . . . "In all thy ways acknowledge Him, and He shall direct thy paths!" (Prov. 3:6).

So we have the four principles which can guide you in using the nutcracker technique:

1. Maintain equal force on the jaws. That is, see that your light and your works match. Undue pressure on either is a waste, for the light is pointless without something to illuminate, and your works cannot be seen for what they are unless your light shines on them.

2. Start off gently. Ease into the technique so as not to startle your husband with sudden, dramatic changes and outbursts of light. He may not need them. And you need time to get familiar with the technique. Make your mistakes with the small areas, before graduating to severe pressures.

3.   Take ONE area at a time. This allows you to SELECT the changes you wish to make without concern for the other areas of your life which also need fixing. In this way you can give them your full attention so that the changes are genuine and become a permanent part of your growth process. Also, it lets you bypass those areas of submitting to demands of your husband which would cause you to displease the Lord.

4.   Start away from yourself. Things are easier to change than people. So you begin the plan by making household changes which please your husband. You learn to work with the Holy Spirit as you do these, for there is no threat to you in them and you can talk to Him even as you do them. Then you go to work on yourself, but changing things on the outside before tackling things inside. Your clothing, places you might go with your husband, little inconveniences you suffer to please him are all easier to effect than changes in temper, tongue or mood.

You now have the basic plan. But how does it operate?

A FEW EXAMPLES

Principles are more easily understood when you see them applied to actual situations. I will illustrate the shifts found as you start away from yourself. Once you see them applied, you will be able to picture them at work in YOUR situation.

  Let's start with your dinner table.

Is it ever graced with pots right off the stove? Do hastily opened cans and milk cartons and TV dinners tell your husband you haven't time to fix him a good meal? Your first shift in this area can tell him you are taking pains to see that he is PLEASED at his table. Our first example considers your husband's stomach as an opportunity for the nutcracker technique. He'll respond. Most men have a fondness for food. Isn't that what gave rise to the old saying, **"The way to a man's heart is through his stomach?"** Use it for Christ.

You make a change. Perhaps something as simple as a lace doily under his plate. He sees it:

"Hey, what did I do to deserve this! You'd think we were expecting company or something!"

"CLICK"...

"No, dear. It's just for you. The Lord has shown me what a nice husband I have. This is a token of my appreciation. I'm glad if you're pleased, for the Lord has put a real desire in my heart to please you."

I am only illustrating here. Do not regard this as a specific instruction. Use your own ingenuity. Ask the Holy Spirit's help in selecting items for the nutcracker. It can be a single item that he is sure to notice. When he comments you have something on which to shine your light. It doesn't really matter what the specific change is, so long as he is PLEASED by it and it draws out his comment.

Now it could just as well have been the best china, a new dress you were wearing, or some favorite dish which pleased him. The point is, he SAW IT and commented. You merely explain that it was done to please him — **because of Christ.**

B. Let's see how the principle works as we illustrate a specific change that has to do with your appearance. Again it is just an example.

You've been a rather doudy housewife without too much zip. A little on the drab side, we'll say. And your appearance has matched your mood — dull! You decide upon a change in your clothes, just to please him. He notices. Now your light:

"CLICK". . .

> "Why yes, dear. Thanks for noticing. The Lord is making me conscious of the way I look to you. He wants me to be a more appealing wife. So I am obeying the Lord and you get a more attractive wife!"

Then maybe you take off a few pounds. He couldn't miss that.

"CLICK". . .

> "The Lord Jesus has showed me that it would make my husband happier and more pleased if I took off a little weight. So I did . . . for Him and for you."

Maybe you rise a little earlier to fix your hair before he sees you at the breakfast table. He notices:

"CLICK". . .

> "How nice of you to notice, honey. The Lord Jesus doesn't want me to send my husband off to work with his last picture of me as a frowzy housewife. So for your sake, He has me get up five minutes earlier to fix my hair. If you like the new look, you can thank the Lord." (A big smile goes with this.)

● See what is happening? You could work on one specific after another until you had yourself in shape as a sharp looking woman. But that is only a by-product. As each improvement brings forth a comment from your husband, you use it to squeeze the nutcracker a little more. Once you begin this plan, EVERY CHANGE becomes an opportunity for the nutcracker.

C. Now we come to your **person.** This is the hardest area, but it is the most effective. He will appreciate the changes he sees here, so will the Lord. They prepare you for **Him,** too. By now you have learned to trust the Holy Spirit as you went to work on a specific change and clicked on your light. So you are ready for these changes in yourself. You can see why it has been best to approach them gradually. You need time to get used to the technique in the power of the Spirit.

Wondering how to go about selecting a personal change? Obviously your worst fault would be noticed quickly if you made a change. But I can't ask for that. Besides the human ego has a built in defense mechanism which keeps us from seeing the worst in ourselves. It's a good thing. We'd all shoot ourselves if we didn't have that. Even if I asked, "What do you think is the area where you fail most in your submission to your husband?," it would be hard to answer. But should I turn it around and ask, **"What specific area in your life would he be likely to notice if you changed or improved?"** Something would come to mind.

● Are you a complainer? He couldn't help but notice when you stopped. Has he ever accused you of being careless with the family income, spending too much time on the phone, or paying too little attention when he is speaking? Faults accumulate when living with a man. Start thinking about things he'd notice were you to change, and you might come up with a list of items for the nutcracker.

When it comes to HUSBAND-PLEASING changes, it can be just as startling to do something you haven't been doing, or abandoned years ago. Things like meeting him at the door with a kiss, with a whiff of perfume behind your ears, or laying out his slippers and pajamas across the foot of the bed. How about those cuddly kisses before bedtime? Have those long since gone?

"That's the last thing in the world he needs!"

Oh, oh, did I say the wrong thing that time? Let's discuss it.

We are talking about **pleasing** a man. This is what the FEMALE script calls for. And we're after **noticeable** changes. Any woman who can please her husband sexually and make it clear that Christ has brought him this pleasure, has that man firmly in the jaws of the nutcracker. It has ever been Satan's plot to kick Christ out of the bedroom, but you can defeat him.

No doubt I have picked one of the hardest areas to illustrate the personal change, but it is worth mentioning, because of its tremendous husband-pleasing quotient. I don't wish to over-emphasize the sexual part of marriage, but neither do I want to be misunderstood. So we will take a little space for it, if only for the sake of the nutcracker technique.

Changes in the sex area.

Sex is one of the most powerful, emotional features of married life. It ought to be harnessed and used for Christ where one is married to an unsaved man. Any Christian who fails to please her husband sexually . . . and on top of that refuses to let her light shine in this area . . . fails not only her husband, but her Lord. As delicately as I can say it, I am suggesting that you deliberately help your husband to soak in sexual satisfaction and then — **with equal force** — let him know he owes his pleasure to Christ. Dear wife, this is a powerful technique. The Holy Spirit is able to use this mightily when it is done sweetly and in His strength.

> **NOTE: Some husbands, due to their emotional makeup, can respond to this with excessive vigor. Your desire to please is not to carry you into disgusting sexual acts. Should your husband get carried away, simply refuse to participate in that SPECIFIC ONLY. Do not let it keep you from entering into that WHICH YOU CAN DO, with all your heart.**

● Sex is a big thing in a man's life. And a wife can use it for a mighty squeeze when her submission is made "as unto the Lord." God Himself installed sex as the BASIS of marriage . . . "For THIS CAUSE He made them MALE and FEMALE." That's about as frank and primitive a statement as can be made on the matter. But here is what I want to have perfectly clear . . .

I AM NOT TALKING ABOUT MEETING ALL THE NEEDS OF YOUR HUSBAND.

I am not even hinting that you should go all out in meeting his demands. I am speaking of a CHANGE in the way you go about giving what submission you do give. Putting it bluntly, I mean quality rather than quantity. Please don't be offended. I sincerely seek to help you serve Christ and win your mate.

You know what happens to sex in marriage. It's an old story. A couple drifts into an adjustment where the wife learns her husband's MINIMUM needs and then gears herself to MINIMUM SUBMISSION. Feigned tiredness, headaches and calculated timings are used to keep her from giving more of herself. Well, if it has to be that way, let it be. But I must observe that meeting needs in a man is not the same as PLEASING him. We should face it. No husband is honestly pleased with a wife who simply learns to TOLERATE his sex needs.

● Pleasing and tolerating are two different worlds. Often adjustments serve only to heighten the male appetite. Why? He tries to compensate for his ego-frustration by increased sexual demands.

The CHANGE I have in mind relates to the wife's ATTITUDE. Regardless of how often she feels she can submit to her husband, it is the WAY SHE DOES IT that counts. It could even require a **special anointing** of the Holy Spirit for her to bring pleasure to her husband as she uses the sex-area for Christ. In which case she should ASK the Holy Spirit for it. He is extremely faithful to give this kind of help. After all, is the Spirit's help any less needed to reach a lost husband than some other lost soul? That wife who will harness this powerful sex area as a means for reaching her husband, can count on God's Spirit to back her to the limit.

Let a wife submit herself to her husband "as unto the

58

Lord," (a delightful experience in itself), and he will notice the difference. What is that difference? The **quality** of her submission. She is hearty and joyous. She actually PLEASES HER HUSBAND as the Holy Spirit (the Director) has asked her. Her eyes are on HIM as she gives her best to the part assigned her. I am telling you now that ANY CHANGE AT ALL will be noticed by your husband. This area is too sensitive, too critical, for **any improvement** on your part to be overlooked.

When your mate comments, let your light shine:

"CLICK"...

"I'm glad you are pleased, darling. But I can't take the credit. After all the Lord has been showing me ways to be a better wife. It is because of Him that I want to please you. If you feel like thanking someone, thank Him!"

There—a pleased husband with the wife giving Jesus the credit. That is WORKS AND LIGHT combining for a mighty squeeze. And in one of the most critical areas of marriage. Am I asking too much? Shocked that I would even suggest using sex for Christ. Then hear God's Word on this very thing:

"Whatsoever you do in word or deed, do it heartily as unto the Lord and not unto men . . ." (sex included!) (Col. 3:23)

Has Satan been allowed to dominate our bedrooms? You bet he has! And if you have to take a nap in the afternoon so as to be a fresh and responsive wife, do it. You won't be sorry. Besides, it's great to be a woman—very much alive!

These illustrations give an idea how the nutcracker technique works—you please your husband and then give Christ the credit.

NOW LET'S REVIEW THE FORMULA AS JESUS GAVE IT:

a. **LIGHT.** Your light is your word which tells your husband that Jesus is responsible for the change he has noticed in your life.

b. **WORKS.** Your works are changes made in your daily life which please your husband as you carry out the submissive role in the marriage drama. You make the changes you feel the Lord would have you make, limited to those things which He can approve. Pleasing your Director, the Holy Spirit, has priority over pleasing your husband.

c. **SEE.** Inasmuch as you openly credit the Lord for the changes in your life, your husband is forced to consider Christ as the cause. Until you credit the Lord, your husband is free to praise you, dismissing your works as merely his good fortune in having a fine wife.

d. **GLORIFY.** God is glorified the moment your husband becomes aware of the Lord's working in his own home. Whenever a heathen is confronted with the truth of Christ and forced to consider Him, while a servant of the Lord testifies to His presence, God is supremely glorified. Down inside your husband is saying to himself, "The Lord really is working in my wife." This inner acknowledgement brings God's glory to your home.

If you go one step at a time, you can't get into trouble. You submit only where you have liberty in the Lord. The moment your husband comments on ANY KIND OF A CHANGE, you have him in the nutcracker. All that remains is openly crediting the Lord Jesus. The Holy Spirit takes it from there. Actually the technique is quite simple.

SIMPLE?

At least the principle is. Doing it can be hard. But it can also be fun. How much fun depends on how intimate you become with the Holy Spirit. It is His power that squeezes the jaws of the nutcracker. The more you learn to work with Him the more exciting it becomes to squeeze your husband . . . for Christ!

A lady came to see me about her unsaved husband. **"I'd give anything if he could be saved,"** she said. But you know how easy it is to mouth those words. So I exposed her to the Nutcracker Technique to see if she really meant business or was merely voicing a longing. Of course, it was new to her.

Her face registered surprise and amazement as I took her through the truths of, **"No Marriages in Heaven."** She had always felt that there was a certain man for every woman. Now she learned it didn't make any difference whom she had married. She was playing a part in a drama and just who the MALE star was didn't affect her role at all. That is no slight truth in itself. But this was a test. So I let her have it all in one sitting — not in chapters as you're getting it.

One of her hardest gulps came when she learned that her role in the marriage went **beyond** meeting her husband's needs — she **was to make him happy.** It staggered her that this was a Christian assignment from the Lord, perhaps more important than anything she could do at church. She was a churchy Christian and summed her service for Christ in terms of activities at church. When I told her that her home was the center of her private world, and that was where the Great Commission was sending her as a missionary, she was stunned. She was a generous giver to missions, but was overlooking the one heathen she was truly responsible for.

She absorbed the truth. She meant business. She really wanted her husband saved. I asked if she would be willing to allow the Holy Spirit to use her and employ changes as Gospel bait in her own home. She was willing, but admitted that serving as **personal** bait was a new idea. We took out pencil and paper. She struggled to write down everything she felt the Lord would have **different** in her life. When it was her turn to pray, she asked the Holy Spirit specifically for His help and presence. His witness was immediate.

As she was about to go out the door, she turned and said:

"Dr. Lovett, for the first time in a very long while, I can hardly wait to get home!"

The Spirit of God had already planted the thrill of working with Him in her heart.

A week later she returned for a follow-up interview. Did she ever bubble! Radiantly she told how the Holy Spirit had shown her exactly where to begin and what to say to her husband. She had made changes. Her husband had commented. When she gave the credit to Jesus the power of the Holy Spirit went into operation. Rapture filled her soul the very first time she tried the technique.

In incident after incident she had seen her words penetrate her husband's spirit while the Holy Spirit bore witness. She found she could read the responses in her husband's face. She rejoiced as HE used her to reach her husband. It was exciting for her to watch the Spirit squeeze him:

> "The thrill of working with the Holy Spirit in reaching my husband has gone beyond anything I ever dreamed. I don't know what it is for other wives, but it hasn't been a chore for me. I think I've finally discovered what the abundant life is all about . . . dealing with people in the power of the Spirit!"

I was glad to hear that. It is not easy to get people to see how much easier it is to use technique in the power of the Spirit than the flesh. Honestly, though, it cannot be done any other way, as you will see. Next.

Radiant—in the power of the Holy Spirit!

Chapter Five

SQUEEZING!

Earlier I mentioned our method of teaching Christians how to witness. It's called the LADDER-METHOD as found in our book, "Witnessing Made Easy." Can you guess why it's called that? A ladder permits a person to reach a height in small steps he couldn't reach in one jump. It breaks up an otherwise impossible distance into convenient gaps. One can do easily with a ladder what he couldn't possibly do without one.

This method starts witnesses off with no contact with strangers. People scare people. Secret exercises are taught first to build inner strengths before there is any face to face contact with prospects. The closer you get to people the more threatening witnessing becomes. Let a witnessing student stay with the first steps until he is comfortable and he will find himself ready to try the harder ones. A ministry which at first seems impossible isn't hard at all when approached gradually and in easy steps.

We do the same with the NUTCRACKER TECHNIQUE. You start with easy actions before attempting hard ones. When it comes to a wife's submission to her husband, there are some types of submission easier than others. We begin with these to gain strength in preparation for the harder ones.

THE FIRST SUBMISSIONS

As mentioned in the last chapter, the easiest changes have to do with your surroundings. Changes **in yourself** are a harder type of submission. These should be deferred until you get used to working with the Spirit of God. Since the technique depends on His witness within your husband, you must learn to work with Him at close range. To live with a man and see God's Spirit work on that man as you apply your technique, will be brand new to most wives. Consequently you are doing more than acquiring pressure moves. You are learning the science of cooperating with the Spirit in an intimate situation. The mastery of this science doesn't come overnight. Therefore your first changes, your first calculated submissions, will be of the type which do not present too much threat. An overdose of threat could keep you from seeing what the Holy Spirit is doing. You will be too worried about yourself and what your husband might do.

Is there a housekeeping chore you dislike? Of course. Does this tend to make you lax about it? One wife may hate to iron her husband's shirts, another to keep house. Or maybe your sink is perpetually full of dirty dishes? If so, your husband has surely remarked, **"Honey, do we always have to see a stack of dishes on the sink like this?"** That's something to work on. Would he notice if you changed the procedure and kept the sink spotless? He would? Good. Do it and when he comments . . . "Click" . . . on goes your light.

For instance.

Let's make it something as simple as fixing your husband's coffee. We'll assume you have been using instant coffee because it was easier to make. Yet all along you could tell he preferred fresh-brewed. Would he notice the change? And how — particularly if you accomplish the change-over with a bit of fanfare—like this:

You make the coffee just the way he likes it. Then you unplug the coffee pot and hold it in front of him with one hand while you fan the aroma toward his face with the other. He can't miss that! A whopping smile on your face invites his pleased reaction:

"Hey! Don't tell me we're going to have real coffee for a change? How come?"

"Click". . .

"Well, it's not only because you are such a good husband. I've been asking the Lord to help me be a better wife. He put it on my heart to do something just to please you. So . . . courtesy of Christ . . . you will now get fresh brewed coffee every morning!"

How simple that is, and how pleasant. Your works are illuminated by your light. There's no threat involved. Your

Oh that smile — in Christ

husband is pleased. Christ gets the credit. And whether your unsaved partner likes it or not, Jesus is the One responsible for the fact he will enjoy fresh brewed coffee each morning. Your husband is squeezed between your works and your word. He is delighted and Christ is glorified. The nutcracker is working.

> NOTE: That example shows how you can take almost anything from your routine and turn it into a nutcracker incident. It didn't have to be coffee. It could have been the location of his favorite chair, or who empties the waste basket in his study, or any of a number of items wives can change to please their husbands. It need only be something he is sure to notice and elicit his comment.

But we're not through with our exercise. As soon as you say those words to your husband, your light is "clicked" on. It shines fully on your works. Your husband's likely reaction is a bewildered . . .

"Oh?" He doesn't know what else to say. He is pleased, yet startled.

A sweet smile creases your face. His comment cannot be hostile, for you have just served him and pleased him—

with delight. No one gets angry at that. But don't say any more. Give your light a chance to do its work. Turn away. Carry the coffee pot back to its place. As you walk away from your husband, silently lift your spirit . . . **"Bless those words, dear Lord. And bless my husband too."**

> NOTE: You have stepped out of the picture. Your husband is left with your words lingering in his ears. The Holy Spirit has a chance to ignite them. You ask and He does it. See how a non-threatening action like this gets you started with the technique? You have nothing to fear. You get the "feel" of the plan. And you start getting acquainted with the Holy Spirit as an action-Partner. You speak, He works!

THE HOLY SPIRIT'S PART

I will mention the LADDER-METHOD of witnessing again. You should know that every step of that plan is designed to teach the student the thrill of working with the Holy Spirit at close range. Two basic elements make this possible: (1) The first movements are so simple the beginner scarcely needs to think to carry out the action. (2) There is little or no threat, releasing him from all concern of what others might be thinking. If these two features are not present, a brand new witness is too occupied with himself to see the Spirit in action. He is actually **blinded by pre-occupation with himself.**

Since you are out to win your husband for Christ by means of the Nutcracker Technique, it is at once a method of witnessing. Therefore these essentials of the LADDER-METHOD must be a part of the plan. Your first actions must be so simple you barely have to think of what it is you want to say. And they must be so free of threat, you don't have to worry about what your husband might be thinking. Without this kind of freedom, you will not be able to concentrate on the Holy Spirit. From the very beginning of this plan, you must be FREE to WATCH HIM WORK. Once you see Him in action, your confidence soars!

God's Spirit is ready to take ANY LIGHT/WORDS you utter and anoint them to a prospect's heart. Your husband is your prospect. Upon request, the Holy Spirit will seize your words the moment they leave your lips and plant His witness in your husband's heart. This is something you can SEE, **if you're watching** and are not required to explain your actions. In other words, if your action is very simple, offering no threat, you can relax and watch the Spirit use your words. In time you will get used to reading the signs in your husband's face. Then you will know exactly what the Spirit of God is doing with what you say. But that too is something which doesn't come overnight.

With that, let me now suggest that all of your squeezes with the nutcracker should be experiments in the power of God. You must be satisfied that HE does precisely what I am telling you. Once assured He backs you with power, you will have amazing confidence when you try the harder actions. Later, when you will be making dramatic changes in your life, the Holy Spirit will be your strength. Perhaps now you can agree that a plan based fully on the working of the Holy Spirit can't miss!

HUMOR

Humor is an important ingredient to any witnessing plan. It has the power to strip threat from almost any situation. Can one laugh and be angry at the same time? No. If your first actions contain a little humor, they will be almost free of threat. And the SMILE is the prime means for easing humor into a conversation. Smiles pave the way for chuckles. Chuckles give way to laughter.

Your husband has been complaining about the appearance of the dinner table. Your schedule has become so hurried you practically eat out of pots and pans. A milk carton sometimes graces the table instead of a pitcher. Sometimes there are no napkins. Yet, when company comes for dinner, the table is very different. It is prepared with your finest. He has remarked about this.

Set the best for your husband. Again attach a little fanfare — for the sake of humor. Make a crude paper crown for your husband's head. If that's too much, draw one on his paper napkin and label it . . .

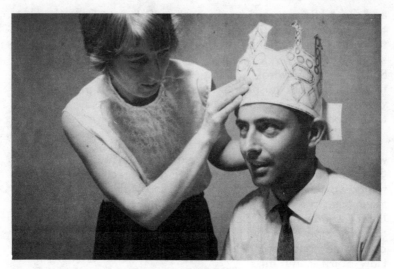

Long live the king — for Christ!

"King John (or whatever his name is)!"

He'll see it. He also looks over to your smiling face. He can't
help but say something. When he does . . .

"Click". . .

> **"Well honey, that's part of my wife improvement plan. Every
> time I talk to the Lord Jesus about you in prayer, He reminds
> me that you are the head. So I thought this might be a nice way
> to let you know I'm glad you are!"**

He gets the message. You needn't say more. In fact,
right after those words you should be chatting with the
Holy Spirit. On the surface it sounds as if such lines do not
carry much witnessing force, but they do. Even the Alphabet
has power when the Spirit of God anoints it. Does your husband feel the squeeze? Sure. But does he get angry? No.
How could he? This is humorous. Also, you have announced
him as king. That can only please him. Ah, the subtlety. He's
king . . . **courtesy of Christ!** That's the message he gets.

● Is that preachy? No. Neither is it nagging. Well, not unless you want to call the whole technique a form of nagging. Your husband is scheduled to run into all kinds of surprises informing him that the happiness he finds in his home is due to Christ. Think of the effect this will have on him in time. Before long it will occur to him that not only is he living with one of God's chosen servants, but the very joy of his home comes from Christ. How much of this can an unsaved man take before reacting? That's what makes the nutcracker effective, there is a breaking point. Each man has a limit.

> **NOTE:** Though you acknowledge his kingship in this manner, it is only with respect to his TITLE. There is no way to give an unregenerate man total mastery over your life. Later, when you fail in some area of submission, he may throw it back in your face that he is the head of the house and king. Should this happen, USE IT. Simply acknowledge both . . . "Yes dear, even though you are king, I'm a miserable subject. When I pray for you, I will also pray for myself that the Lord Jesus will help me to be a better wife to you." That way, even your failures are turned into witnessing squeezes.

Every time you squeeze your husband with a LIGHT/WORKS action, determine ahead of time to be very sweet. Smile and add a dash of humor wherever possible. While humor strips threat from a scene, your smile does even more. Actually, it is your armor!

A SMILE IS ARMOR?

Yes. And you need armor. Down inside, your mate feels the sting of these frequent encounters with Christ. Those stings are painful. There is hurt as the Spirit pierces his soul with your words. Inwardly, and at first secretly, he would like to strike back. If you were anything but sweet, he would. Many times he would rather have you sarcastic, so he would be justified in ridiculing or even striking you.

69

But what man allows fury to overtake him when his wife is outwardly making every effort to please him? And the more so when she appears to be happy about it. That's what a smile does. No husband wants to retaliate against someone who smilingly and cutely makes him the head of her life. A husband won't allow himself to become enraged at such a nice wife. Who then? That leaves just the Lord. If he is to take his feelings out on someone, it will have to be the Lord Jesus. His dear wife is so nice to him, so sweet. Her precious smile indicates nothing is wrong between him and her. To be angry with her, would be like getting mad at himself. That leaves the Lord as the target for his surging feelings.

That's what you want. Your sweetness and humor do more than avoid unpleasantness between you and your mate. They actually turn him in the direction of Christ. There is no other target. If he wishes to retaliate, it will have to be against the One Who has called you to be a submissive wife. See how urgent it is for you to maintain Christian tenderness, displaying only loving concern for your husband? No matter what he says or does, you are the gentle, submissive wife . . . **"Yes dear."** That is your power!

● Not only is this Scriptural,* but it keeps you out of the way. You must not get between your husband and the Lord. If you do or say anything that causes a duel, you become the target and Christ is hidden. Satan must not be permitted to lead you away from your role as a loving and submissive wife. If you cannot submit to a specific act, your spirit must nonetheless remain submissive — certainly passive. If you behave in any other way, you step out of character and ruin the scene. So no matter what your husband might do — **don't react!** You are an actress, not a re-actress!

DON'T REACT?

Yes, dear wife. Those two words hold the secret of success for the nutcracker technique.

*1 Peter 3:1-6

As you continue squeezing your mate, his suffering increases. In time he must react to the pressure. Hostile words finally issue from his mouth . . . **"You're not going to start that again, are you?"** or **"Do you always have to bring the Lord into everything we talk about?"** Please understand this is normal. He is behaving according to plan. So expect it. Worry only if his reaction **doesn't occur.** Be glad he feels the pressure and it shows. The point, though, is **that you are not to react.** If you do, it can ruin the action. It cancels the squeeze.

> HINT: There will be times when you WILL REACT. You are not expected to execute this plan with no failures, for it is also a plan for bringing you to maturity. It is important that your failures not be allowed to distress you. Don't get mad at yourself for your failures. They are expected. And Satan, with his usual cunning, knows how to exploit them. If thoughts such as, "Now you've done it!" or, "How can you expect to make this plan work when you are such a failure?" arrive in your mind, dismiss them. All a failure can do is make you more alert and teach you what to watch for. They can't hurt you, unless you buy Satan's suggestion that you are a failure, and can't hope to win your husband by this method. Remember: A failure cancels only one scene, it does not ruin the whole play!

You will recall we devoted an entire chapter to the truth that marriage is an earthly drama. It is a play with male and female roles. We have come to a place where it is helpful to have this as a working truth. You put the squeeze on your husband. He reacts. That's what you want. But you do all you can to keep from **reacting** to his words or threats. I want you to continue acting your part regardless. He is doing exactly what is expected of him—**reacting.**

You've heard of Dr. Charles E. Fuller, the radio evangelist and seminary founder. He's with the Lord now. But a few years ago, Mr. Dewey Lockman, Dr. Franklin Logsdon, the famed Bible teacher and former pastor of Moody Church, and I went to see brother Fuller. We were scouting for scholars to serve on our committee for the New American Standard Bible. In the course of the conversation, the name of a prominent Christian leader was mentioned. One who was then attacking Fuller seminary. shall never forget brother Fuller's response to the comment this man made about his school:

"Yeeesss," he drawled, **"God bless him."**

Dr. Logsdon was the quickest to respond, "You don't seem too upset, brother Fuller?"

Then came an astonishing reply: **"Why should I let someone else decide how I am going to act!"**

Silence followed that. The three of us felt something astonishingly Christian had just occurred.

What was it that made Charles E. Fuller ACT instead of REACT? He was a settled Christian, secure within himself. As I faced him across his desk, it seemed his spirit was totally serene within him. He was completely self-possessed. I could feel the power of it. Apparently it didn't matter what went on around him. Externals seemingly didn't bother. He refused to return evil for evil, for to do so would mean that he was no longer in command of himself. I was watching a Christian giant behave as the master of his own conduct. It was beautiful.

● Coming home in the car my mind rehearsed that scene. The word ACT was jumping within my spirit. This man of God had ACTED. He didn't react. I thought how often and how quickly I reacted to people and circumstances. I even blushed a little, inside. For a time the Holy Spirit bounced my soul between those two words . . . ACT . . . REACT! I needed that lesson.

THE STORY FITS

That incident fits beautifully into the nutcracker technique. A wife in command of herself ACTS toward her husband. One who is **not** self-possessed, REACTS. And no one is unhappier than a **perpetual** reactor. You've seen people like that. A little praise and their spirits soar. A word of criticism and their hearts sink out of sight. Reactors are good to those good to them, bad to those bad to them. What other people do, they do. What others are, they are. I am overstating it when I say they are like yo-yos, but you get the point.

72

One of the sweet by-products of the nutcracker technique is that you learn to come into possession of yourself. Ultimately, you see, all we really own is our personalities. This is all we take with us when we leave this life. So it is important to our souls, not just our marriages, that we become actors rather than reactors.

Reacting wrecks the scene. When a wife **reacts** to her husband's harsh words, she becomes the target for his feelings. When the squeeze is painful, he emits his criticisms. He is happy when she reacts. He wants her to be the "whipping boy" for his fired feelings.

But how different when she ACTS instead. She is no longer his target. He must then lash out against the One directly responsible for his pain . . . Jesus! That's the finest fruit of this technique — getting your husband to face Christ. When you learn how to make your husband mad at Jesus, **instead of you,** you will be a master of this technique. Once he directs his rage toward Jesus, the Holy Spirit has him. You see it is hard to find fault with Christ. All He has done is give your husband a lovely home and a sweet, submissive wife. God's Spirit takes those feelings and turns them around with convicting power to crack the shell of his resistance.

SUCCESS OVERNIGHT?

Hardly. One cannot shift from a "re-actress" to an actress overnight. But you have a comforting advantage. Since you are following a plan, you know **ahead of time** that your husband could react to your pressures. You can anticipate and be ready. In fact, if you set yourself for the worst, it can take the sting out of almost anything he might say. It is ADVANCE PREPARATION for **his** reaction, that helps you to ACT your part in the drama. Quiet talks with Jesus make you disposed to look on your husband as the "star of the show." They prepare you to live with his tempermental displays.

I do not expect you to become a polished actress in a week or in six months. Neither is it necessary for you to revamp your entire personality. The plan calls for you to go one step at a time. You need only to be ready for each reaction to specific nutcracker incidents. Since you know WHEN you are going to make a pressure move, you need only to be ready for the one reaction which flows from it. That's not the same as asking you to change your whole personality.

In time, of course, you do become a better actress. You watch yourself change. You become more self-possessed. What your husband does and says has less and less effect on you. After all, should you remain a puppet, dancing when he pulls the string? The Holy Spirit is the Director of your life and He is bringing YOU to maturity as you play your role. The more polished you become as an actress-wife, the more mature you become as a Christian.

FINALLY . . . yourself.

Changes in yourself include such things as temper and tongue, patience, attitudes and moods. Just naming them shows the wisdom in beginning with things AROUND you, before attempting changes WITHIN you. It's not easy to change your own personality. Are you not more sensitive to criticisms about your **person** than the way you keep your yard, for example? That's why we begin with externals and graduate to the personality changes. Sensitivity is something we are to overcome as we reach for maturity.

Women can develop careless habits unintentionally when living with a man becomes routine. The longer they have been married, the more these habits accumulate. Even in the matter of habits, there are some outward changes to be worked on first. It is easier, for example, to rise a few minutes earlier to fix your hair so that his first sight of you is refreshing, than to hold your tongue when he remarks about your disintegrating figure. You may not like getting up early to fix your face for an unregenerate man. It may gall you to appear on the set each day as fresh as a daisy. But for whom are you doing it?

The Director asks you to **please** your husband. Would you sacrifice a few minutes sleep for Him? Of course. So you rise early. You prepare yourself for another day before heaven's cameras. All actresses make that sacrifice. You look lovely. Your hair is nice, no flannel bathrobe is draped about you. You're serious about your career in Christ. Maybe a whiff of perfume scents the air as you walk by. Prefume? In the morning? Sure, why not? You make your own rules. You are out to win a man for Jesus. This is the language he understands. Won't your husband notice? You bet he will!

This is what I mean by **outward** personal changes. These are external changes that have to do with you as a person. But now we come to those changes deeper inside your personality.

● Are you already a patient wife? Many are not, especially when they suffer continual disappointments and indignations from a heathen husband. Does it bug you when he delays dinner? Are you extremely irked when he says he'll be home at a certain time, but it is obvious he doesn't care whether he makes it or not? Such a situation is an opportunity for the nutcracker. Does your husband sometimes keep you sweltering in the car while he chats with his cronies? Do you mark time while he makes idle conversation on the phone? In that interval, be thinking how you are going to display a new patience and use it in the nutcracker. Oh oh, here he comes now. Listen to him, would you. He even sounds guilty. He knows he should have returned from the neighbor's sooner. He knew you were waiting to go:

"Sorry I took so long, but we got to talking. . . ."

"Click". . .

"That's all right dear. It gave me a chance to talk to the Lord about my patience. You provided a situation where I could have gotten upset, but I discussed it with my Lord. He reminded me that I am to be a submissive wife. So I didn't mind waiting. The Lord Jesus is teaching me that my time is your time."

75

"Wow!" He may do a double-take at that. But he gets the message. He's off the hook for being late, because you belong to Jesus. Once again Jesus has made a rough situation smooth. He is faced with Christ at work in his home once more, making things more comfortable for him. Well . . . they would be comfortable if he didn't keep running into Jesus all the time. But that's the point. There's his precious wife acknowledging her time is his. Can he get mad at that? No. Yet she just squeezed him.

Observe that this is NOT a change in your overall patience. It was but **one** display of patience, a single instance. You are **not** calling your husband's attention to the fact that you are a changed woman. You simply used a demonstration of patience for the nutcracker. Why did I stress this? I don't want you to think that total revision of yourself is needed to squeeze your husband. Maybe last time you were not so patient. But this time you were. And it gave you something you could use.

Now here's another personal change . . . **worry.**

Ever stew over bills, health, your children, your husband's job, the kind of a neighborhood you live in, the pastor, etc.? Your husband, we'll say, is familiar with your worry pattern so a CHANGE would show up big. But we must make it specific.

● A phone call from school reveals your boy has gotten into trouble. Your husband is due home from work shortly. You have a few minutes to prepare yourself. There's going to be a change in your usual worry pattern. Your husband is so used to your upsets, he couldn't help but notice a lack of worry in this crisis. This time you are not only going to banish worry, but use the lack of it for the nutcracker.

(1) **You go to the Lord.** You assure yourself He has an answer for the situation. You sense the crisis fits His plan and at the very least, He will give you the wisdom necessary to meet it. With that confidence only one thing remains before your husband gets home. Deal with the one who usually turns your worry tendencies into torturous anxiety . . . Satan!

(2) **You deal directly with this enemy.** He has already started to gnaw at your mind with . . . "What if this? What if that? What will people think?" Familiar with your weakness, he knows how to inflict such mental agonies. Then they show up in your speech and your behavior. Your husband has seen them often enough. True, he doesn't know of Satan's power to manipulate your thinking and torture you with such questions. But you do.

This time Satan doesn't get away with it. You resist him as the Word of God instructs you.* You deal with him directly in the power of Jesus' Name. He flees from you just as the apostle James said he would. You have learned that prayer is Godward, but resisting is Satanward. For many it is a new experience to deal directly with the devil. But not for you. You have done it before. You do it NOW! There's the release! Those haunting ideas are gone. You smile in the Spirit. What a joy to do something like this in the Master's Name!

● Your husband arrives. Ordinarily he would be greeted by a tearful wife, wringing her hands as she spilled out the calamity. But this time he is met by a self-possessed woman who calmly relates the story as though it were an item on a news broadcast. Of course the problem is serious. It kindles your husband's emotions at once. But you have the advantage. You have dealt with your feelings and your enemy in the power of the Holy Spirit. God's presence is your calm.

---

*Let someone begin a serious action for Christ and Satan immediately offers stiff opposition. Consequently this book makes frequent references to our ingenious enemy. Executing the admonition of James 4:7 ("Resist the devil and he will flee from you") requires some skill. You will be interested in the author's book, "Dealing with the Devil," which presents a simple, four-step plan for effective resistance. It really works.

You speak slowly, deliberately, showing no undue concern. It's as though someone else had already taken care of the matter . . . which of course HE has! Then your husband speaks. Let him say whatever he likes. Take your time in commenting or answering his questions. Your appearance is one of settled assurance. As you look your husband in the face, talk silently to the Spirit of God. He keeps you at ease. There is a settled peace which is easy to maintain if you don't let your words out too fast. Measure what you say. Go slowly. Choose each word carefully. It is your **deliberate calm** your husband must see right now. He does.

"You don't seem to be too upset by this. I thought you'd be climbing the walls by now. What's come over you? Have you had something to drink?" (People in the Spirit are often accused of this. Unbelievers think such strengths come in a bottle.)

"Click". . .

"Well I've had time to talk to the Lord about it. I am assured He will give us all the wisdom we need to handle the situation. I've asked Him to give you the kind of wisdom I can follow, for you are the head. You make the decisions. Besides, why should I worry when I have a Lord Who has the answer to any problem that can come along!"

You can see that it is one thing to SAY the Lord has the answer, quite another to ACT like it. Many brag of their confidence in Christ, but oh how they behave when a crisis hits. Here you are bragging about Christ . . . IN THE SITUATION. You are calm. You display confidence in Jesus in the middle of the crisis. That's what counts. Your behavior shows you truly believe God has the answer. That's why you are worry-free. Your lack of worry is the specific WORK on which you shine your LIGHT.

Does your husband feel this? In an emotion-packed crisis like this, he is guaranteed to feel the squeeze. Not only is he rocked by the news from school, but he is confronted with a miracle in his wife. He is staggered. In the midst of his bewilderment your testimony (LIGHT) penetrates his heart. Perhaps this is the very moment the Holy Spirit has been waiting for. Your husband's shell could crack in a crisis—if you use the nutcracker.

NOW LET'S GO BACK TO THE SEX AREA

We've mentioned patience and worry as deep personal changes. But, now let's return to one more intimate and sensitive. It deserves chapters, so important is it, and so critical. Sex is a fantastic thing rightly used for Christ. But alas, even in some fine Christian homes it is often an adjustment. In Chapter Four we mentioned it is not uncommon for a Christian wife to discover the minimum requirement of her mate and then set herself to live at that lowest sexual level. What is probably the most glorious ministry of the Christian wife is reduced to a tolerated inconvenience.

I said before an entire personality change isn't necessary to make the nutcracker technique work. So let me observe that ANY IMPROVEMENT in your sex moments can be used for Christ in this technique. Anything you can do to PLEASE your husband in the sex area, whether satisfying praise or provocative submission . . . and it is a NOTICEABLE CHANGE . . . consider it a **work** and turn on your **light.**

Let's suppose your husband's appreciative comment is:

> "Darling, what's come over you? You're the same girl aren't you? You make me feel like I've been with another woman!"

He's happy about it.

"Click". . .

> **"I am another woman. Or at least I will be when the Lord gets through with me. He wants me to please you. I want to please you. Between the Lord and me you might end up with a wife who can be ALL women to you!"**

He'll respond to that. His surprise may come out like this:

> "But I always thought of your religion as a sort of wet blanket when it comes to sex. You mean the Lord wants people to enjoy each other sexually?"

79

"Click". . .

> "Why not, He invented it. And He has never yet given us any-
> thing evil. It seems a shame not to ask His help in enjoying it.
> That's what I'm doing. I expect the Lord to make me a better
> sex-partner just to please you. Any way, doesn't it make sense
> that the One Who designed it ought to be able to show us how
> to extract the greatest joy from it?"

Dear wife that is power! You have demonstrated a
CHANGE in an area where no man can help but notice . . .
and be impressed. Your change is your WORK. And now
you shine your LIGHT in an area where Jesus is usually
banned. You'd be shocked to know how many otherwise dedicated Christians refuse Christ any place in their sex-life.
That is downright ingratitude, seeing HE gave the privilege
in the first place.

Can you see how your LIGHT shining here gives
the Holy Spirit one of the most powerful facts of life
to use in reaching your unsaved husband? When you
learn to minister to your mate sexually, you sharply increase
his chances of being saved. Why? You are touching his spirit
at the very root of his being. Maybe you didn't know that the
sex-experience (certainly the excitement of it) is closely akin
to the spiritual experience? It's true. This is why Christian
young people sometimes become sexually involved while
attending intense religious conferences. The feelings in their
aroused spirits are so kindred to the sex feelings, the latter
are triggered inadvertently.

TOTAL SUBMISSION NOT REQUIRED

> "I don't know what to do. My husband wants me to . . . and I
> don't think I should. I don't feel right about it. I know I am
> supposed to submit to him, but there are some things a person
> feels she shouldn't do. Where do you draw the line?"

Wives frequently ask that. They wonder if total obedience
to their husbands is required. And if not, how do they know
where it stops?

● Quickly I will state that God does not require any wife
to give TOTAL OBEDIENCE to her husband. Total obedience

belongs to God alone. In this book I am not insisting on **total anything.** The last thing I would counsel is complete submission to an unregenerate man. I am satisfied the Christian wife should give SOME SUBMISSION "in all things," but total submission — never! Certainly she must not exalt the wishes of a heathen husband over those of her Lord. That is unthinkable.

Who knows what a pagan partner might ask of his wife? With the spectrum ranging from cooperative church-goers to savage enemies of the Gospel, sex demands of an unsaved husband could go from disgusting perversions to outright violations of God's Word. That fact alone should make us give up any thought of total submission. Beyond that, there could be illegal and criminal demands to which no godly woman should submit.

Well then, how do you know what to do?

Bear in mind that marriage is an earthly drama. Serious, life-consuming, yet still a drama. The Holy Spirit is the Director and your part is performed as UNTO HIM. This truth is urgent for keeping things in their right perspective. It can guide you in your choices. Squarely in the middle of Paul's teaching on marriage and the wife's submission he announced a remarkable principle:

> **"And whatsoever ye do, do it heartily as unto the Lord, and not unto men"** (Col. 3:23).

If you are asked to do something which you **cannot do as unto the Lord,** refuse. The Director of your life is God, not some fallible man. His orders have the priority. The star of the show must never be allowed to countermand the orders of the Director. Ah, but **when you must refuse,** even that can be a WORK on which to shine your LIGHT. Let's say such a moment has come. You cannot do as your husband asks. You maintain your sweetness toward him even as you take your stand:

> **"Honey, as you know I am doing my best to be a submissive wife because the Lord asks me to. But that means I am actually trying to please two people, you and the Lord Jesus. Now some-**

times what pleases one does not please the other and I have to make a decision. But since I have to live with Him forever and I will only be with you a short while, I must refuse what you ask. I am really sorry to disappoint you, dear, but you can see when you put me in a place where I have to choose between you and Christ—I am forced to please Him, though I know it disappoints you. I'm sorry it's that way, but the Lord is the One to Whom I must finally give account for my life."

● It isn't so hard to say that, with the Holy Spirit helping you. There is a peculiar thrill that goes with taking your stand in Christ — if you are sweet about it. You see, you are always sweetly **submissive** — but now it is toward the Lord instead of your husband. It's the same submission, but given only to Jesus . . . the One with the priority. So that's how you know what to do. All that is needed whenever there is a doubtful demand made on you, is to ask yourself . . . **"Can I do this heartily as unto the Lord?"** If you can, fine. Submit to your husband. If you can't, don't do it at all. Submit, instead, unto the Lord and refuse. In either case, whether unto your Lord or your husband, **"Do it with all thy might!"** That is the kind of submission that pleases both God and husbands!

"But what if I just don't want to do what he asks?"

Ah, that has to be the real question. That brings us to the heart of the matter. You see, it is not usually a question of whether the Lord approves of your husband's demands or not, but whether you are willing to **obey?** Quite frankly, if you are not willing to obey, there is nothing I can do about that. I can only observe that the heavenly Script asks you to PLEASE your husband with OBEDIENCE — whether you like it or not.

There is nothing in the Word of God which provides for your preferences. The husband is the head and that's that. All that concerns you is the one question:

"Is my husband's demand something I can do as unto the Lord?"

If the answer is yes, then it matters little how you feel. Since you are asked to do it as unto the Lord, you should and heartily at that. When it comes to overcoming your personal unwillingness, that is something for you to admit and work on. This book is NOT designed to make you willing. It is based on the obedience you ARE WILLING to give. That's all that is useful in reaching your husband for Christ. I might mention that the salvation plan is based on a similar willingness . . .

"Whosoever will may come."

The nutcracker technique **does not require** total submission in all things — toward God or your husband. It simply uses what submission you are willing to give. For me to write a book setting forth a plan which could be cancelled by unwillingness, would be folly. We are all unwilling at certain points. So wherever you **are** willing to submit, we can use the nutcracker for a healthy squeeze.

INCREASED SUBMISSION

Let's assume you know the Lord wants you to be submissive, even though you find it difficult. And for those wives who are openly defiant of their non-Christian husbands, we will assume that down inside they too know what God expects. The marriage plan just won't work without feminine submission to the masculine headship. So let's agree it is God's way and labor the point no further.

We move next to the fact that every Christian wife reading these lines has room for improvement in her submission to her husband. It is in the area of **improved** submission that we can also find WORKS for the nutcracker. When I say improved, I mean **some** improvement, not **total** improvement. I do not ask for a revamping of your character which turns you into an obedient wife. I am asking only for SOME INCREASE in your submission — some change in your obedience to your husband's desires — which can be a specific work on which to shine your light.

 We'll suppose your unsaved husband has been wanting you to go to the boxing matches with him, but you have steadfastly refused. You don't care anything about them, calling them brutal and bloody. He has expressed disappointment that you don't share his interest. What would his reaction be should you ask:

"Are you going to the fights tonight?"

"Of course."

"Would you like me to come along?" Your smile goes in place as you look into his eyes.

"Do you want to?" He's puzzled.

"If you want me to."

"But I thought you hated the fights. How come now all of a sudden you're willing to go?"

"Click". . .

"Well honey, being a good wife keeps me on my knees. As you know, I've been asking the Lord to show me ways to please you. I admit I don't know what you see in the fights, but it is important that I please you. So if you still want me to go I will. If it pleases you to have me with you, you can thank the Lord. He's the One making it possible for me to go."

There, that's a sample of what I mean by improved submission. You would do this because he WANTS YOU too. Technically, according to the Script, his wish is your command. If there is something he would like you to do, and it is not contrary to the will of God, then you can interpret it as a desire of your Master in heaven. It doesn't have to be something like going to the fights. The same would apply to spending less at the beauty parlor or for clothes. Or if he asks you to buy beer and cigarettes for him at the market. Does he show displeasure when your friends keep you on the phone for long chats while he is at home? Should there be a showdown between you and him over . . . "gulp" . . . getting rid of his mother-in-law — it would be increased submission if you did it, and heartily. He'd be shocked at the change and your light could shine.

See how it works? Find some matter of obedience where you have been self-willed in the past and make the change

—SUBMITTING CHEERFULLY. That's what makes it noticeable. When he comments . . . "CLICK" . . . on goes your light. Now that's not total obedience, is it? You even pick the specific change you are going to make. You surrender to the Lord in the matter to secure His anointing. Then you turn around and give **cheerful** submission to your husband. The thrill is doing it in the power of the Holy Spirit.

Ever confronted yourself with this Scripture:

> **"I can do all things through Christ which strengtheneth me!"** (Phil. 4:13).

Put it to the test . . . in a single action. In a specific matter. Prove God and press your husband at the same time! It can be exciting. That raises a question? All right, let's have it:

> **"Suppose I go to the fights with my husband. Do I have to go everytime he wants me to, after that?"**

If you can. It would be nice if that question were thrashed out with the Holy Spirit even BEFORE you speak to your husband about going. At least you could be prepared in your spirit to go with him for a time. Why? Once you tell him you are willing to go with him because of Jesus, every time you accompany him **after that,** he senses he is enjoying the company of his wife, courtesy of Christ. You don't have to repeat your LIGHT dialogue each time. Often you can do this with your eyes. A glance tells him this sweet submission is due to Jesus.

It's fight night once more. This time he asks you:

"Going with me tonight, Honey?"

Pause. Wait a bit before answering. Look him in the eye. Fix your smile. Then:

"Do you want me to?"

"Sure. I like having my wife with me."

"Okay, then I'll go. And I'll ask the Lord to help me enjoy it even more than I did last time."

NOTE: Since you are making this submission as unto the Lord, you are submitting to two people. Your husband and your God. So do this heartily, give every indication of having a good time. Why? Because the fights have become somehow enjoyable? No. You are with your husband and he wants to be with you. You are pleasing him. Let your attention be directed to him. Hang onto his arm. Show some bounce, some vigor. When he asks how you enjoyed the fights, reply: "I liked being with you!" The Holy Spirit will help you put zest into it. Anyway, it's more fun being an enthusiastic Christian. Everyone likes enthusiasm — your husband too. The technique calls for him to ENJOY his wife.

How long does this go on?

In time, say six or seven outings, the novelty of your going wears thin. It isn't quite as exciting for you to be there as it was at first. At least you sense you have extracted nearly all the spiritual pressure from the submission you can hope for. You have gone with him and it has counted for Christ. Now he is beginning to take your going for granted. It's not the squeeze it was at first. It's time for a change. You are about to STOP GOING. And stopping can be used in the nutcracker too. Here's the scene. It's fight night again. He asks:

"Will you be ready to go pretty soon?"

"I'm not going tonight, dear."

"You're not! How come?"

"Click". . .

(The answer involves a new principle which I want to reserve for the next chapter.)

Even though you don't know what was said in the LIGHT above, you can see that staying home is also a specific action. Your refusal to go can be a work. And you can illuminate it. When your husband learns WHY you are not going, when he hears that it is because of Jesus that you are staying home, the nutcracker will be in operation. He will be squeezed by your refusal to go with him, but this kind of pressure is of a different order than that which we have been discussing in this chapter. That's why

I am reserving it. I mention it now only to show that you are NOT committed to an indefinite program of going to the fights . . . or whatever specific is selected for increased submission.

The point is, that in the power of the Holy Spirit which makes it possible to "do all things through Christ which strengtheneth" you — you can INCREASE your submission. You can do some HUSBAND PLEASING you haven't done before. And when you do, it becomes a specific work on which to let your light shine. There are all sorts of squeezes a wife can give her husband — if she will take God at His Word — and submit in the Spirit!

So — whether you go to the fights or refuse, you can squeeze your husband. That's the beauty of having a plan of action. You can make everything count for Christ.

SUMMARY

I'd say the most exciting feature of the nutcracker technique is that it works. But next to that, is the happy fact that you don't have to be a completely changed woman to use it. Accomplish ANY specific change which pleases your husband and you can squeeze him. Let him react to an improvement in your personal submission to him, credit Christ for it, and he's in the nutcracker. That's how simple the basic plan is.

The pressures on your husband increase as you make more and more changes. They mount as you increase the frequency of his encounters with Christ. But anything is hard to do at first. So the plan calls for changes in your surroundings and routine before you attempt any in yourself.

You begin with appearances before tackling your personality. Obviously it is easier to improve your clothes, freshness and figure than to change your habits, control your temper or modify your moods. However, you will be able to make SOME change in all these areas since you are approaching them one step at a time. It is the principle of ONE SPECIFIC CHANGE at a time, that puts this plan within the reach of every wife. What wife cannot make SOME improvement? That is all that is necessary for using this plan.

Starting off slowly permits you to get acquainted with the POWER of the Holy Spirit. Most Christians enjoy His PRESENCE, but operating in HIS POWER is a new science for the average child of God. It is like entering another world to find the Spirit of God anointing words on your own lips. To watch your words penetrate a man and do a spiritual job before your eyes, is a brand new way of living. It has to be approached gradually. Why? These workings of the Spirit are so subtle they are easily missed. They appear in the face of a prospect. Starting slowly lets you LEARN HOW to read your husband's face. In time you can read those signs as the Spirit pierces his soul with your words.

Whenever you make a change, perform it heartily as unto the Lord. Let no improvement come with a grudging spirit which says, "I'll do it if I have to, but I won't like it." That is self-defeating. Gain the most for yourself — CHANGE AND LIKE IT. Submit first to the Holy Spirit and HE will **help you like it.**

You can relax. I am not asking for your TOTAL SUB-MISSION to your husband, only HEARTY SUBMISSION . . . and that where you can give it. Discover the power of your personal tools — your smile, perpetual sweetness and a dash of humor. The Spirit of God is eager to be your strength. Use your tools, your surrender, in the power of the Holy Spirit and your husband will squirm as you squeeze!

Polish your part. Be a good actress. Don't let the male lead throw you off balance by anything he does or says. Keep your eyes on the Director. He watches every move you make. Daily you will make changes into the likeness of the Lord and your husband's shell will crack. Isn't that worth doing? You bet it is!

Chapter Six

WHEN YOUR HUSBAND FORBIDS!

"It seems like everytime you get with that bunch of fanatics down at your church, you come home so full of nutty ideas, you're hard to live with. I don't think I want you to go any more!"

Oh-oh!

Has it all sounded simple, fairly easy so far? Seldom do things go as planned. The technique would not be complete unless it provided for harsh reaction. Some men balk. They plant their heels, rearing up to assert the male ego. Their hostility can take the form of forbidding the wife to go to church or have fellowship with other Christians. What then?

Should a wife submit to her master and stay home? Should she cut herself off from Christian contacts as he demands, or should she defy him and go anyway? Not a few women face this. The question is critical. The answer cannot be glib. Just how to use the nutcracker in that situation deserves a chapter to itself.

Let me say this. The technique always remains the same, but now you are faced with a choice. That's what's new about the situation — **the choice you have to make.** Therefore this chapter sets forth principles which can help you in your decision. Once you understand them, you will be able to make a good decision when faced with the prospect of . . . **obeying or defying.**

What you seek, of course, is to know the will of God. Therefore the principles I will give, are those for determining God's will in a particular situation. Naturally they would be useful in other situations. There are marital problems apart from the nutcracker technique where you often yearn to know the will of God. They will help you here also. They are a bonus for taking the trouble to master the husband-squeezing plan. But we need to cover some ground before we get to the principles. So you'll meet them later in the chapter.

LET'S CREATE A SPECIFIC CASE.

Your husband has bought a boat. He wants to spend his weekends on the water. Naturally he thinks you should be with him. With only his weekends free, it gripes him to think you prefer to spend that time with Christians instead of him. He's been steadfastly resisting the Gospel. Your technique has been getting to him. You suspect he has bought the boat to compete with your commitment at church. Maybe you're right. He knows full well you are deeply involved with your church when he comes out with his demand . . .

"I don't think it's right for a church to come between a man and his wife. I only have the weekends and I want to spend them with my wife. How about cutting down on your church to spend a little time with me. In fact, I would like very much for you to come to the lake with me this week instead of going to church. How about it?"

What to do? You're faced with a decision. Let's move according to plan. The plan before you has four steps.

STEP ONE

GO! This is an obedience step, a husband-pleasing action. But it is also a WORK. Therefore you can turn on your light.

"Click". . .

> **"I do like being with you Honey. And if it will make you happy, I'll go with you. After all, I am trying to please the Lord with my life and He wants me to bring pleasure to you. So let's go see what that boat will do!"**

> NOTE: This comment is made sweetly, without a tinge of regret. It has the tenderness of a devoted wife, plus the excitement of sharing a new toy! Give your full approval to his plan. Do nothing to dilute his joy. It is no credit to Jesus if you are a wet blanket or display a sullen spirit. You have just credited Christ with wanting you to please your husband, so be a good companion. Maintain your vigor as an exciting wife. Let him thrill to your company. Later, when his resistance to the Gospel may cost him this fascinating woman, you won't be sorry. That's part of the plan.

● You can make a number of comments similar to the one above. The first, naturally, is when he asks you to go. Since the Lord wants you to please your husband, you tell him you are willing, **because of the Lord.** Perhaps another opportunity comes as you are driving to the resort area. Again, perhaps, when you are out on the water enjoying the boat. Afterwards, he will ask if you had a good time, at least, what you thought of the boat. Don't over do it, but purpose to get in three Christ-crediting comments. It'll take about that many to exploit a situation properly.

 Now you are home from the outing. You are having a cup of coffee together before retiring. It's then he asks, "Pretty nice having something like that, isn't it? We're going to have a lot of fun with that boat." The Holy Spirit will use your eyes now. Look directly at him as you move in with the reply. He's felt the sting of your anointed words before:

"Click". . .

"Sure it's fun. But even better, I like being with you. It's great doing things together. But I need to find a way to maintain my Christian strength. The Lord wants me to be a good wife to you, but it is Christian strength that makes it possible. And that means I've got to be in Christian fellowship as well as be with you. If I can live up to all the Lord expects of me, I'll be the best wife you ever had!" (Smile.)

What about next Sunday?

He's ready to go again. He wants you to go too. Should you? Yes, if you will click on your light, say four or even five times. And you can plan on going with him the following Sunday as well. In fact, as long as you can make it fully known to him that he is enjoying your company because of Christ, go. And with each passing week, increase the comments some.

> HINT. Alert your friends at church. It will help them to understand what you are doing. Some might even be offended if they don't know you are carrying out a plan. They might be led of Satan to think that you too have gotten excited about the boat and traded your fellowship with them for it. Don't react if some criticism comes your way, for it might get back to you that some have accused you of putting your husband before the church. You can head it all off by letting the right people in on your plans.

It may develop in time, say after four outings, that he begins to chaff under continued references to the Lord and how it is Christ Who is making it possible for you to have a good time with your husband. The day may arrive when he suggests:

> "If you're going to keep that up, maybe it would be better if you went to church and I took the boat out alone!"

It won't be easy for him to say this. You have demonstrated enthusiasm for him — and the boat. In fact, it will be very painful. It means that deep inside he has had to decide to forgo the company of his charming companion because of the Gospel. You can see that the more vigorous and enchanting you have been, the harder it is for him to reach this decision. It amounts to a showdown within his own spirit.

● So what do you do when he says this? Go back to church. And feel perfectly at ease about it. It should be no shock to you when your stand for Christ separates you from an unsaved person — your husband included. Remember what our Master said of Himself in this very connection?

> **"I am come not to bring peace on earth, but a sword . . . and a man's foes shall be they of his own household"** (Matt. 10:34-36).

When your light is shining, it will surely separate you from those **"who love darkness rather than light"** (John 3:19). The more brightly shines your light, the sooner this reaction is likely to occur.

Ah, but what if your husband learns to adjust to your words? Suppose that even though he feels the keen edge of your witness, he manages to shrug it off by closing his heart somehow? And instead of getting upset, he appears immune to your flashes of light? What then? How long do you continue to forsake your church for him? Well, I cannot prescribe a time limit, but the principle is this:

> **As soon as you see your LIGHT/WORKS combination is no longer effective, stop going with him. When the novelty of your going has worn off, so has your witness. It is the thrill of your being with him and being able to credit Christ for it that makes the going a nutcracker incident. When going is routine and no longer a pressure move, it's time to stop.**

● What about a compromise? What if he suggests you go with him every other Sunday. Then you could have your church and him too. All right, go. But each time you go TURN ON YOUR LIGHT and increase the intensity with each outing. If you fail to illuminate your work, you are wasting your time. And this could happen if you find you prefer to be with your unsaved husband rather than God's people. But that's up to you. This plan is based on the idea that you want to see your husband saved and are ready to pay the price.

STEP TWO

You've been going with your husband every week. Let's assume the fifth week has rolled around and he's going to ask you again. But you conclude you have extracted the maximum witness from this kind of submission. You can tell that your LIGHT and WORK combination has become somewhat routine. He has adjusted to it. With their usefulness past, you feel it is time for the next strategy. What is the next pressure move?

He mentions the outing. It's time for your announcement:

"Click". . .

> "Honey, as much as I love to be with you, I must get back to church. It's been great getting out with you these past weeks, but the strength to be the kind of a wife I should, depends on my spiritual condition. To be in top spiritual condition, I have to be in fellowship with God's people. I've told you this before. It is because of my spiritual relationship to Christ that I want to be a good wife to you. To be the wife I should, I need the spiritual re-charge I get at church!"

> "Okay, if you have to. But it won't be the same without you."

> "I know dear. But there's nothing to keep you from coming with me. If you enjoy having me out on the boat, think what fun it would be for me to have you at church. It works both ways. I could enjoy my church a lot better too, if I could share it with you, just as you enjoy the boat better with me along. Why don't you think about it?"

● You return to church. No matter how he pleads, you sweetly refuse. You are careful to keep it clear that being the kind of a wife you should depends on your return to church. You imply that he is the one who gains by your going. So every time he asks you to go, you carefully . . . "CLICK" on your light. You lovingly explain WITH LIGHT just why you can't go with him. That's what makes it a pressure move.

94

Is this hard on you? Yes. I won't deceive you about that. But you may be assured that WITHOUT YOUR PERSISTENT PRESSURE, he will not change. He doesn't have to. You don't want the same situation to drag on for years. And it will if you do not keep your plan in steadfast operation.

A little showdown.

Once Adam had to choose between God and Eve. He chose Eve. She was so lovely, so exciting. He couldn't stand the thought of being separated from her. Satan used those powerful feelings to woo Adam from God. But now you are reversing the process. You have become a thrilling, exciting woman to your husband. You are going to use his natural affection and passion for you as a means of wooing him to Christ. Confront him with a choice. Make it between his rebellion against the Gospel and companionship of his fulfilling wife, and it will pain him to let go of her. He is more apt to abandon his hostility, than let go of an exciting woman. At least that is our strategy. We know we're on mighty ground, for anything that could make Adam defy God has got to be powerful. Why not use it **for** Christ?

He begins to change.

You notice a difference in your unsaved husband. He's beginning, we'll suppose, to manifest a grumbling discontent with boating by himself. Little things tell you he is unhappy over your church-life. Sarcastic remarks indicate his displeasure is about to erupt. You have not been asking his permission to go to church, you have just gone. And you keep on going. You want the pressures to build inside him. You wait for his reaction. You will be ready for it and will use it. Then the eruption you've been expecting comes . . .

"You know, I've got some rights around here. I pay the bills. And doesn't that Bible of yours say I am the head of the house? Besides, since you live under my roof and eat my food, it seems you ought to do what I say. Doesn't your church teach you to obey your husband?"

"Something like that." A nice scene is building. You sense he is going to tell you not to go to church any more. So you say as little as possible. The last thing you want is a debate with him about who is head of the house and who gives orders. It's better to agree with him. In fact, you can hardly go wrong with the two safety words . . . **"Yes dear."** He comes out with it.

> "All right. Here's what I want you to do. You're not to go down to that church any more. I'm tired of having half a wife. You are going to forget all this church stuff and settle down and be the kind of a wife you should — or else."

Don't bother with the or else. You don't care what he means. He's emotional and doesn't really know what he means either. What is important is that you have come to step three. And you are ready to set it into motion.

STEP THREE

His remark doesn't bother you too much. You smile a little—**inside.** An outward smile would be infuriating. He's serious about this. He thinks he's hurting you. He wants to. You've been paining him with your LIGHT/WORKS and he's finally erupted. He doesn't know that you have been waiting for this and he is going to receive MORE PAIN through your staying home.

You are prepared to stay home. Your close friends at church have been notified of your plans and are praying for you. You will be digging harder into your mate in this step so prayer support is an urgent resource. He means to hurt you, but you will pain him. You have already made it clear you cannot be the kind of a wife he wants without spiritual recharging. He knows that fellowship with God's people is part of it. Even so he orders you to stay away from church and remain with him.

"Yes dear."

Then Sunday comes. In order to flash your LIGHT, you need his command to stay home once more. So you **extract** it by asking,

"Do you still feel the same way, dear? It's Sunday and I wasn't sure the other day whether you were upset or really forbidding me to go. What about today? Can I go?"

"No, I don't want you to go."

"Click". . .

"All right, honey. I'll stay home. In the Bible the Lord Jesus teaches that you are the head and I am the body. So I will obey you and stay home because the Lord Jesus wants me to."

NOTE: Now you make sure you use the fuller title of the Master, the Lord Jesus. Inflect a bit as you say that Name. From now on all of your actions are due to the Lord Jesus. As you emphasize His Name in your dialogue, it will bite deep into his spirit. Again and again he will hear that his wife is being submissive because of the Lord Jesus. His needs are being cared for because of the Lord Jesus. His wife is obedient because of the Lord Jesus. At every turn he runs into that Name. And each time it pierces his soul — with pain!

Another Sunday comes. You ask again. He is adamant. "No. I told you I don't want you to go." He thinks he is wounding you deeply, but he is the one suffering the agony.

"Click". . .

"Yes dear. I'll stay. I'll obey you the best I can for the sake of the Lord Jesus. I must please Him and it pleases Him to have me do as you ask. And as long as I feel my Saviour is pleased with my obedience to you, I'll do what you ask."

CAUTION. Don't preach. Avoid all phrases which suggest, "Why don't you accept Christ so we can go together?" Do not say to him, "How different it would be if we were both Christians, etc.!" That's preaching. You are NOT to preach, just shine your light. All that is required of you under this plan is **turning on your light** (not God's) to **expose your works.** You are not to witness to this man until he comes to you. I have reserved that for Chapter Eight. If you preach to your mate, you step out of your role. Let God's Word alone when it comes to your husband . . . other than to say what the Bible tells YOU to do . . . not your husband. Later you'll see why.

Keeping up the pressure.

Watch your church's calendar of events. Ask permission to go when there's a meeting of some kind. Not that you care to go to every single meeting, but each event provides an opportunity to ask his permission. Every time he refuses, you have submission on which to shine your light. I'm not saying you need to jab him for each meeting, but you could if you wanted to. Then there are subtler occasions:

1. When the church-bulletin arrives in the mail.
2. When someone calls to tell of an exciting meeting or outing.
3. When the sermon title appears in the newspaper.
4. Ladies groups, missionary circles, special speakers etc.

With these you can say, **"Oh how I wish I could go. . . ,"** Or, **"I wish I had been there. . . ,"** Or, **"My how I would love to be there and hear that!"** Each is something you would like to attend but cannot because of his prohibitions. Each time he refuses to let you go . . . AND YOU STAY HOME . . . it is a work. You are obeying him. Each instance is a specific act of submission. Every time he says no, click on your light. The intensity increases. More and more you bring it up, feeling your way carefully to make sure the Spirit is working with you as you apply the pressure. Plan each move. You know ahead of time you are going to ask, so chat with the Spirit. Ask Him for the sweetness and calm needed upon each refusal.

NOTE: You can see I am describing the maximum effort. What you will actually do in your own situation depends on your personal strengths for facing your husband. This will determine how often you can squeeze him. The tendency of wives is to shy away from squeezing as often as they should. They fear his reaction and for good reason. The pressure is terrific.

NOTE: Sweetness and surrender on your part cannot drive your husband from the Lord unless he is ALREADY DISPOSED to rebellion. So don't think you can ever be responsible for what the nutcracker technique produces in him. What you do is no more responsible, should he turn away in final apostasy, than the rain is responsible for what comes up in the ground. You can only bring out what IS ALREADY THERE!

Personal safety.

If your husband is a violent man, given to rages and temperamental outbursts, you might have occasion to fear for your safety. Therefore I will leave open the matter of how often and just when to apply the squeezes. You and the Holy Spirit will have to decide the timing. But the notion I would build in you is this — the harder and more often you squeeze your husband, the sooner the matter of his salvation will be settled — one way or the other. It would not be right for me to insist that you follow a plan which could bring harm to you. Therefore reserve for yourself the precise moments for using the nutcracker. However it does take pressure to work. You must keep building the pressure to get the desired reactions from him. And we have been thinking of what it means to him to make you stay home from church.

"Click". . .

> "My, I'd love to go to that meeting. I'm sure it would strengthen me to be a better wife. But since you forbid it, I won't go. I want to do what you ask. I want to please you as long as I can. Because I know it pleases the Lord Jesus to have me please you. You know it is because of Him that I am obedient to you."

Another time your words might ring differently:

"Click". . .

> "All right dear, I'll stay. I love to please you, doing as you ask, but the Bible also tells me I should be in fellowship with other Christians. The Lord Jesus has made it clear that His people are to be together. I feel terrible bringing this dreadful responsibility on you. Here I am causing you to go against the Lord. I'm so sorry, dear."

— Or —

"Click". . .

> "It's terrible to be such a pest to someone you love, but I must ask if I can go. The Lord Jesus expects me to do my duty and I have a responsibility to do what I can to obey His Word as well as obey you. I hope you understand that I love you and have the greatest desire to fulfill your wishes. So it is to please the Lord Jesus that I must ask you if I can go today. I'm sorry if it is an inconvenience, honey."

. . . again . . .

"Click". . .

> "I don't mean to wear you out, darling. But I'm in a hard place. I'm trying to obey you and please the Lord at the same time. You know how often I have told you the Lord Jesus wants me to please my husband. Because of my desire to please the Lord I must ask if I can go, and in my desire to please you, I'll stay home if you tell me to."

. . . another time . . .

"Click". . .

> "Sweetheart, please don't be angry with your pesky wife. I love you and it is hard trying to please two people — you and the Lord Jesus. My repeated requests to go to church are my obedience to Him, just as staying home all these times make up my obedience to you. You shouldn't be upset when you see I am trying as hard to please you as I am the Lord. I love you both."

You could make up a thousand more once you get the hang of the technique.

The increased pressure is working.

> "Honey, do you think I might possibly go tonight?"

> "Are you going to start that again?"

> "You don't know how sorry I am to have to ask you, my dearest. I feel terrible that my obedience to the Lord Jesus annoys you so. I wish I could do something to ease the pain for you. It's no fun for me loving a man and being a pest at the same time. I can only guess that you feel an awful burden of responsibility before God by now!"

NOTE: See that? You now begin to plant the idea of his being responsible. Psychologically he will start to associate the repeated "Nos" as his burden, **not yours.** You explain that it is your responsibility to ask, but the decision is his responsibility before God. At first this doesn't seem so heavy, he laughs it off. But in time he starts thinking he has much to account for. Also, your sweetness gets sweeter. You squeeze harder, his burden is greater. And your spirit shows you pity him and the awful burden he bears. Ugh, he hates that.

Then the needle goes deeper . . .

> "Oh Honey, I feel so sorry for you. I wish there were some other way. But here I come again asking if I can go. And of course your answer will be no. I feel awful adding another weight to the burden of responsibility you already bear in this matter. It must be a staggering load by now. But what's worse, my darling—I'd hate to be in your shoes!"

> "Oh? Why?" You catch him with that.

Something new is added to your technique. You wait until his responsibility-burden is well developed before you use it. Then you thrust the Sword of Truth deep into his spirit. There's power in what you are about to do next — awesome power.

THE WARNING TECHNIQUE

The answer you give his query deposits a barb in his soul . . .

"Click". . .

> "Well dear, I hate to tell you this. But God can play rough. These past weeks when I have stayed home on your account . . . well . . . every time you said, 'No, you can't go.' the hand of the Lord was raised higher against you. The Lord Jesus has been watching our marriage very closely. And while He is a patient Person, there is a limit to what HE will ask me to bear. I don't pretend to know what that limit is, exactly . . . but you could be in danger this very moment. The wrath of God hangs over you and the patience of God could end any second!"

> "What are you talking about?"

"Click". . .

> "Just because the Lord Jesus hasn't done anything about your hindrance of my spiritual life until now, doesn't mean He will ignore it endlessly. It only indicates that He is patient, giving you every chance to act as you should . . . on your own. But there is a point where He may have to get rough with you, and I mean rough."

> "Rough, how?"

"Click". . .

"Well, no one can say exactly what the Lord Jesus will do with a person. Maybe it will be in connection with your job or an accident in the car. Perhaps a sickness such as cancer or something will happen to one of the children. But it will come Honey, you can be sure of that. And when it does, it won't be nice. It will probably affect all of us. Oh my dear, I'm sorry to see all this come on you and not be able to do anything about it. Yes, I'd hate to be in your shoes. (Pause.) It could even happen today!"

NOTE: The key words are . . . "I'd hate to be in your shoes." They have the effect of transferring the full responsibility to your mate. Also they make him feel isolated . . . targeted . . . already under the judgment of dire consequences. Once those words leave your lips, two things happen:

1. The Holy Spirit is then in a position to deal with your husband in a new way. He can start sending tragic acts into your husband's life, ranging from a flat tire on the freeway to a serious sickness. What will God use exactly? We don't know. But HE will begin the tenderizing process by means of external blows.

God never sends tragedy (or uses it if you prefer) without light. Once your husband understands God is ready to deal with him, the Spirit is in a position to USE THAT MEANS. And the acts can range from angry words with his boss to an auto accident. You can only mention the GENERAL AREAS, God alone knows the specific acts required to penetrate your husband's spirit.

What is important is seeing that you have placed the Spirit of God in a new position. HE can send these specific hurts into your mate's life and he will know WHY THEY HAVE COME. That's important. Those acts must count or God will not use them. God will not use misery unless it does a job. When the blows fall, your husband will understand them as coming from the hand of an offended God. And you will be there to interpret them.

102

2. Your husband is in a new position. Until now he would probably not credit God for an overt act occurring in his life. Likely he would refer to anything that happened to him as "just an accident," or, "a bad break," or, "tough luck," using any one of a number of the world's expressions for explaining life's bumps. But now it is different. He is going to view EVERYTHING that happens to him . . . from a broken shoe lace to dropping a wrench at work . . . as coming from the hand of the provoked Creator!

● You make all this possible with your LIGHT. You plant the suggestion that God is going to deal with him with a heavy hand. The Spirit witnesses to this **internally** as the events occur **externally.** When you plant the suggestion, you give the Spirit something He can use. You are working with Him at close range. As soon as you turn on this light, the Spirit will be ready to lower the boom on your mate. Once your husband understands that God is ready to use a little FORCE in reaching him, there's MUCH the Spirit can do. In a sense you untie God's hands by preparing your husband for this OUTWARD working of God in his life. And you do it with LIGHT.

Then what?

You wait—and watch.

● Four forces are currently at work in your husband. (1) Your perpetual references to the Lord Jesus as you give sweet submission to your husband. (2) The inner witness of God's Spirit that your husband is opposing God. This brings painful conviction. (3) The external workings of God as HE arranges events and incidents to confirm your words. (4) The mounting pressure within your husband with each passing day.

These combine to bring results. Can such agony go on indefinitely? Something must give way. But which way? Will your husband become further embittered, hardening his resistance into irrecoverable hostility toward the Lord? Or will his defiant spirit yield in wondrous submission to the Lord Jesus? Wait. You'll know before long. There's a breaking point in everyone. Apply enough pressure and anything gives way — even the earth's crust which has the scars to prove it. We call them volcanoes.

● Step number four is drastic. As we approach it, we will assume your husband has successfully resisted the pressures of step three. He has not exploded in rage. In fact, there has been no eruption at all. Instead, he has become grumpy. He subdues the bitterness within him and somehow manages to reconcile himself to the LIGHT/WORKS squeezes. Usually a hobby, but in our supposed case the boat, permits him to exhaust his rage. In any event, he manages to ventilate his feelings away from home. He now needs something more drastic than any treatment received so far.

WHAT'S NEXT?

Before I present the drastic action of Step Four, another matter must be raised. How long should you wait before you advance to this more severe step? Just when do you move to step four? Now you must do something, there's no doubt about that. But when? How do you know when it is time? I won't answer precisely. As I did before, I will give you a Scriptural principle that will help you know when it is time. You and the Holy Spirit can make the decision together when you use this principle. The Lord Jesus stated it:

> **"Give not that which is holy unto dogs, neither cast ye your pearls before swine . . . lest they trample them under their feet and turn again and rend you"** (Matt. 7:6).

The Pearl/dog principle.

Does it shock you to think of your unsaved husband as a "dog" of Scripture? That's exactly what he is as far as the Word of God is concerned, as long as he remains an enemy of Jesus. Any unregenerate wears that title. But what you are wondering is how can he be "sanctified" by his believing wife (1 Cor. 7:14) and still be a "dog?" Quickly I tell you he is a "sanctified dog." The word sanctified, as used here, does not mean saved. It only means "set apart for special treatment." It is used in the same sense as the vessels of the tabernacle or the temple. They were sanctified in that they were set apart for special use. In your husband's case, he is set apart for special treatment. He is sanctified for a special working by the Holy Spirit. It is no slight thing to be married to someone eternally joined to the Lord Jesus. It is something special.

Applying the principle to your case.

When your husband is no longer **impressed** with your LIGHT/WORKS submission it is time for a change. When he merely **accommodates** himself to your illuminated submission you know you have extracted the most from the number three step. When he smirkingly puts up with his "fanatic" wife, contemptuously shrugging off her "religious remarks" . . . he can be treated as a scriptural dog! You have sacrificed fellowship with other Christians for this man. If he cares nothing for your works and words, shedding them like water off a duck's back, your pearls are neatly laid in front of a pig. Pigs don't care where they put their feet.

● The Pearl/Swine principle applies to your situation as soon as your unsaved husband is as indifferent to your sacrifice as a pig is to a string of pearls. When he despises your testimony and ridicules your devotion to Jesus, he is like a sow stomping a priceless strand into the mud. You can just imagine a pig doing that, can't you. Pigs can't tell an orange peel from a diamond brooch. The instant you feel what you are enduring and sacrificing for Jesus is being tolerated as a stupid gesture, it's time to think about the next step. When he is merely amused by your devotion to the Lord Jesus you can leave step three.

STEP FOUR

We finally come to it. It's time to defy your husband and return to church.

He says you can't go, but in this step you go anyway. Yet you do so as sweetly as you know how. Even in your defiance of this man, you are a sweet wife. With tenderness and compassion you tell him why you must go:

(Don't think to memorize the long dialogue which follows. I want you to get the gist of it only. Get the FEEL of it.)

"Honey, you know I am working on a program to be a better wife. It's because I love you. I want you to have the finest wife possible. But I have come to the place where I can't be the wife I should without the strength I get from being with Christian people. It's for your sake, dear, and the sake of our home, that I must get back to church.

"You are a fine man. You deserve a wonderful wife. For me to be at my best requires spiritual strength. A woman is not an animal, she's a spiritual creature. I need the vigor and encouragement which only Christian people can give me. So for your sake — so that you will have the kind of a wife you need—I must get back to church.

"The Bible says that you are the head and I am the body. That's what makes a marriage in the first place. So please think of my going to church, not as a defiance of your headship, but in order that you may have a sound body. As long as I felt my staying home could be used to help you find the Lord, I was glad to do it. But now I see that it isn't helping you at all. In fact, it is hurting you. Every time you tell me I can't go, it adds to your responsibility before God. And it hurts me too. It makes me feel that what I am trying to do for you is wasted. You can understand how it would be hard for me to be a good wife if I felt my life were being wasted.

"If we keep on like this, and I feel as though I am accomplishing nothing, it's going to drag me down. I will become dull and drab. You don't want to be married to a pitiful creature and I don't want to be out of the will of the Lord. Besides, if I keep this up, I will end up being sorry. You see I am going to be judged one day too. And on the basis of what I have actually done for Christ. I'm certainly not accomplishing anything glued to our house — nothing for you or for me. So out of love for you and the Lord Jesus, I must go.

"I'm sorry if you feel you have to forbid my going, but I have reached the place where my obedience to God has the priority over my obedience to you. Going doesn't mean I don't love you. I do. I'm going so that you will have a better wife. And you won't be sorry. So remember, dear, I am not going in defiance of you, but in obedience to the Lord. I'm certain you will be happy about it when you find me a happier, more cheerful woman. And I can be that if I maintain my spiritual health. So for your sake — that you might have a wife that is pleasant to live with—**I am going back to church.**"

The words are like honey from your lips. There is no sarcasm. You are sincere. You feel pity for this man. There's no doubt about your being a better wife. It pays to maintain your spiritual vigor, it gives you bounce as a woman. If you don't return to church so as to keep up your spiritual strength, you will become bitter and snap back at your husband. So your decision to get back into fellowship with God's people is not just part of the technique — IT IS A NECESSITY. It is for this reason that you stand on good ground in speaking to your husband. What is urgent about this is the WAY in which you tell your husband you are going. It is your sincerity and gentleness which make it easy for him to accept your defiance. You can feel perfectly honest in telling him it is for his sake — it really is!

ACTION . . . GO!

Don't tell him such things unless you are ready to go. And as soon as you inform him of your decision, act. Return to church. You say he won't let you have the car? All right, let some friends pick you up. But go. Consider now that your going is a WORK — a pressure move. Your explanation for going is your LIGHT.

> NOTE: Counsel with the Holy Spirit before telling your husband you are returning to church. More so, if he is a harsh, belligerent man. Your graciousness is your strength. Meekness on your part is power. If you lose control and engage him in debate, you will move out of the Spirit and into the flesh. Your husband would like nothing better. He'd much rather fight you than the Lord. If you behave as anything but a sweet, tender, loving, devoted wife — you become the target instead of Jesus.

SWEETLY DEFIANT

You maintain yourself as a devoted wife, your speech is quiet, you reflect tender concern. When you keep yourself enchanting and loving, there is no way for him to react against you. That leaves only the Lord as the "thorn" in his side. You behave always as his friend and companion, desiring only the best for your mate. Every move you make is calculated to keep you from thrusting yourself between your husband and the Lord. It is your "quiet and meek" spirit that lets you stand aside while your unsaved husband decides what he is going to do about Christ. If he is going to take out his fury on someone, it will have to be Jesus. That's what you want.

The Holy Spirit has your husband where He wants him.

Your SWEET DEFIANCE causes terrible feelings, they rage through his being. ·This is why you must not get into the act. Never do you scold, berate him or challenge what he says. You make no defense for yourself. Gentleness and meekness are your weapons and he has none to match. You can see that BOLD defiance would instantly turn his attention from Christ to you. Your technique would be frustrated, your plan cancelled. This is why all must be done in the power of the Holy Spirit. Not once have I said this would be easy for you, only that it works.

● To defy a husband, no matter how sweetly it is done, blasts his ego. We take that into consideration. The ego, you see, is the mightiest force in the human organism. Now you are using it as a Gospel tool. When you defy him, this force rages wildly inside him. If there is to be an explosion, it will come now. You have triggered the most powerful drive in his being. Until he finds the right target, it works against him, punishing him. His soul-pain is awful, excruciating. He can't lash out at you, you're on his side. Even your reasons for defying him are for HIS SAKE. This is what makes his fury surge. The pressure builds. Something has to give.

IT DOES!

What will happen now? If your husband **doesn't** explode when you first come out with your SWEET defiance, he will in time. When he does, it will probably go like this:

1. **"I can't stand this any longer, Dear. Tell me what you want me to do. Just let me know what it is. We can't go on like this, I can't take any more."**

That's music. His rebellious spirit is broken. He is ready for a personal encounter with Christ. Of course, what he does with Jesus once confronted with Him, is his own business. But he is ready now to take steps to put an end to the pressures on him. Your persistence has paid off, his resistance has crumbled.

NOTE: This would be the place where we would deal with your husband for salvation. But I want to cover that in a separate chapter, where I can set forth in detail exactly what to do when his spirit surrenders. Only part of the work is done when his resistance shell is cracked. It takes a little know-how to bring your mate to a solid, clear-cut decision for Jesus. And I want you to have what you need should it become your lot to deal with him yourself.

Or, it can go like this:

2. "I've had it up to here with your religion. If you are going to persist in this ridiculous fanaticism, I'm leaving!"

Ouch, that doesn't sound so nice, does it? But that is the other reaction which could follow his explosion. You must be ready for it and weave it into your plan.

READY FOR ACTION

The explosion finally comes. Your husband announces he's leaving.

"Well, darling, I'm sorry. I will miss you so. But if you feel you have to go I respect your judgment. And I will ask the Lord Jesus to bless you and keep you wherever you are."

There. See? You don't react. You were ready for his words. You remain calm and sweet, ready even to turn the situation into still another pressure move. And that, dear wife, is preparation and skill at its best. Does he let that go by without further comment? No sir.

"There you go again with that Lord Jesus nonsense!"

"Don't you want me to pray for you dear? Who knows what might happen where you're going? I love you too much to think of your being out there with no protection at all. I'm going to ask the Lord to forgive you for all the times you wouldn't let me go to church. As long as He holds that against you, I dread to think what might happen to you, Honey. Ugh, I don't even like the thought of such terrible things!"

NOTE: Sounds like we're twisting the knife, doesn't it? Well we are. Did you know that fear motivates people to do right, more often than the promise of reward? It's the fear of getting caught that makes good drivers, not the idea of a perfect driving record. Police cars make us obey the traffic rules, not good driver citations. So plant all the **fear** you can in your husband. The fear of God turns a man quicker than anything else. Yes, quicker than love.

OUCH!

He feels that fiercely. The pain is intense. Will he take a gun and shoot you? Not likely. In every way you have avoided getting **between** him and the Lord. His rage is really against Christ. Jesus is the One Who has caused this trouble, breaking up his home. You have been as sweet as candy all the way. It would be very hard for him to lift his hand against a meekly submissive woman, devoted to him — let alone a gun. What man would strike a woman who seemingly lives to serve him, who praises him to the sky; and still wants the best for him — even in a showdown!

This is why you never answer back, no matter what your husband says. You can see why some women get into trouble with their infuriated mates. Fantastic forces are loosed in such moments and those wives who enter into debate with their inflamed husbands are the ones who get the axe.

"But what if he packs his bag and actually goes out the door?"

The Apostle Paul answers that: "LET HIM!" Or more precisely . . .

"If the unbelieving (husband) leaves, LET HIM LEAVE: the brother or sister is not under bondage in such cases, for God has called us to peace" (I Cor. 7:15).

You couldn't find a clearer Scripture, or one more to the point. Paul unflinchingly says . . . "LET HIM GO!" Don't do anything to stop him. If he is determined to leave, it would be unhealthy if you caused him to stay. It is much better that he leave the house. Besides, he probably won't go far.

 It's no fun for a man to be alone. Given time away from the pressures, he will begin to reflect on the lovely home his wife kept for him and the wonderful way she gave herself to him. It's almost certain he will be back before too long. He had it too good to stay away. If **Christ in you** is really so distasteful to him that he cannot come back . . . well, isn't it better that he stay away? You're not going to give up the Lord Jesus.

● But it could be that YOU decide you can't live without this man. What if for the sake of the children, you feel it is better to have an unsaved husband rather than no husband at all? I have no counsel for that. You will have to seek your own compromise level. It will mean extinguishing your light and settling for a situation which makes it possible for a heathen man and a Christian woman to live together peaceably. If you elect to dim your light in order to live with such a man, I must leave that to your own conscience before God. I am not your judge. Neither will I tell you what you should do. I am only telling you what you **can do** if you want to see that man saved. I furnish the insights, you furnish the decisions.

> NOTE: This book is written to lay out the ENTIRE route a wife could travel in dealing with her unsaved husband. It does NOT tell her how far she should go in applying the plan to her own situation. No two women are alike. What is easily possible for one, might be a nightmare for another. Yet it is important for me to set forth the complete plan for those who can go the full distance in bringing their husbands to a decision. Since the Holy Spirit is the real Author of the nutcracker technique, He is the proper One to coach a wife in how far she should go in squeezing her husband.

SUMMARY

This chapter has presented a four-step plan for the wife's conduct with an unsaved husband when he begins to interfere with her freedom to fellowship with other Christians. It shows how his interferences can be harnessed and made a part of the nutcracker technique. In every case WHAT YOU DO is a work and it is illuminated by WHAT YOU SAY. Whether you stay home or go to church it remains a WORKS/LIGHT operation for the nutcracker. Either way, you are ready to put the squeeze on that man.

Abbreviated, the plan looks like this:

STEP ONE ....STAY HOME

At his request, you refrain from going to church. You do it to please him. This is a work. You illuminate it with words so that he can SEE it is because of Christ that you sacrifice your church-life for him.

STEP TWO ....GO TO CHURCH

He hasn't told you you CAN'T go to church. So as soon as you exhaust the effectiveness of staying home, you return to your church routine. You explain that you must get back into fellowship with God's people. And it is as much for his sake as yours. He will be denied your company. That is what you are using in this step.

STEP THREE ....STAY HOME

He insists you stay with him on the weekend. You do, but asking constantly if you can go. Each refusal highlights the sacrifice you are making for him. This sacrifice is the WORK which you illuminate by saying you want to please him (by staying) and the Lord (by asking if you can go). Each refusal adds to his burden of responsibility for the spiritual damage he is doing to you. Finally, you plant the warning stinger . . . **"I'd hate to be in your shoes!"**

STEP FOUR ....GO TO CHURCH

Now you defy your husband, but very sweetly. You go to church whether he likes it or not, explaining that it is necessary for him and your marriage. Only by the strength received in fellowship can you be the wife he deserves. You behave your gentlest and enchanting best toward him, careful not to make yourself the target of his feelings. You have reached the place where your obedience to Jesus has priority over your submission to your mate. Your timing in reaching this step is guided by the Pearl/Swine principle.

POWER

We close this chapter with a word about spiritual power.

The more intense a situation becomes, the sweeter you must remain. This takes power, the supernatural power of the Spirit. May I suggest that before you set this plan into motion, you first establish some kind of daily intercourse with Christ. This would be a devotional interlude which brings you into intimacy with the Spirit of God, a familiarity which finds you chatting with Him about specifics of the plan:

> **"Lord, You know how easily I pop off and say the wrong thing. Help me to watch my words and be mindful of You every time my mouth is open!"**

Use plain speech in talking to the Lord. It brings Him so much closer. Avoid pious, religious language when you fellowship with Jesus, for the language of ritual shoves people away. It destroys intimacy. Approach the Master as you might a psychologist, who was also your father. Be familiar with Him as a Person, yet awed by His insight and wisdom. As you chat with Him, be confident HE IS going to give you all the strength you need . . . WHEN YOU ASK HIM FOR IT. Like anyone else, He hates to be taken for granted.

> **CAUTION: When you use this plan, DO NOT take the Spirit of God for granted. He will let you stew in your own juice if you do. And you'll deserve it.**

Ten minutes a day would be fine. Try to set aside that much time for Him, though I know the days are hectic in our hit and run type of living. You won't be sorry. And don't concentrate on Bible verses or truths, focus on Him. Get next to HIM — cuddle. Make HIM the center of your devotion, not your Bible. Actually, it is only a tool of revelation. It is the Lord Jesus Himself you must embrace in the Spirit, not just His Word. Yes, I understand how you treasure that Book. I do too.

● Laugh with Jesus, cry some too. Then when the more intense moments of your plan come upon you, you will be ready. The Holy Spirit will nudge and your mind will flash to Christ. Then — as you speak — you will see your words sink deep into your husband's spirit. You will thrill to the engulfing presence of the Lord. How comforting that is! You will find that it is the presence of the Holy Spirit that makes this plan work. In fact, the harder you lean on Him, the more effective it is.

I mention that because we are coming next to something that really takes power. It will be by the Spirit that you will understand my words. What you are about to read in the chapter ahead could be startling. So get ready for a truth that might indeed shock your spiritual sensitivity the first time you meet it. Next.

Christian fellowship is finally necessary. It cannot be sacrificed indefinitely for an unsaved man!

114

Chapter Seven

WHEN SHOULD I LEAVE MY HUSBAND?

"This is my house. I pay the bills around here. I want you to give up this church nonsense and be the kind of a wife I need. I'm not going to put up with this religious stuff. So no more radio programs, no more of your churchy friends coming around. In fact, I don't want to hear another word about your religion, understand? And if you don't like it, well . . . that's just too bad!"

THAT'S ROUGH!

The marriage program is so clearly set forth in the Word, the thought of leaving your husband seems almost sacrilegious. Most Christians don't even want to talk about it. I said you'd meet a shocking truth here. This is it.

Now it is not a hard choice when a husband says, **"Either give up Christ or get out!"** The issue is so sharply drawn you know what to do. God's will is clear. But the matter is not always so nicely packaged. Usually a husband doesn't go that far and the decision is left to you. That's when you ache for counsel. Not a few women are in this plight. They don't know what to do.

If you are not faced with such a situation and do not know anyone who is, you could skip this chapter. Your understanding of the nutcracker technique will not be affected if you do. However, you may want to absorb the principles used in this chapter, for the time surely will come when you will want to know the will of God in another matter, and these principles will help.

LEAVE MY HUSBAND?

Rocks you, doesn't it?

115

 Sometimes the husband just won't leave. It's his house, he says. And if anyone is to go, it will have to be you. He may then attempt to throttle your spiritual life. Going so far as to physically silence you by placing his hand over your mouth or locking you in your room. He might break all the radios in the house and prevent Christian friends from calling on you. You might have to stand by and watch your Bible burned while he smirks . . .

"If you don't like it, you can get out!"

What then? Do you leave? Can you? Is it financially possible? Sometimes a wife may wish she could leave, but pure economics forbid. She has no place to go, no money to get by on. What can she do? If all circumstances bar her leaving, she simply has to find a way to live with the man. At least for the time. Even if she has to turn down her light, she might do so **temporarily** . . . concluding God would soon reveal some other plan to her. In the meantime she would enlist all the prayer support that could be mustered so the will of God would be executed on schedule.

But it is not the lack of finances nor the threat of bodily harm that concerns most Christians. Many devoted ones are ready to sacrifice financial security to be in God's will. More important than food in the stomach or clothes on the back, is KNOWING what **the Lord wants them to do.** For them must be answered: **"Is it in the plan of God for me to leave my unsaved husband?"** That's what concerns us in this chapter.

> **"But to the married I give instructions, not I but the Lord, that the wife should not leave her husband, but if she does depart, let her remain unmarried or else be reconciled to her husband . . ."** (1 Cor. 7:10-11).

SHOULDN'T LEAVE

Paul rightly says the wife should not leave. We all agree. Who expects God to install earthly marriage as a picture of the heavenly marriage, and then write **divorce** into the play.

But notice what Pauls **does** say . . .

"But if she does leave . . . !"

What does he mean by that? Ah, separation. And separation with a view to reconciliation. He carefully tells the wife that even though she removes herself from her husband for a time, she is not to remarry. Paul evidently understands there may be a time when a wife HAS TO LEAVE, but he is not saying, "Get a divorce." Separation and divorce are not the same, particularly when the salvation of the husband is part of the plan.

● Separation as unto the Lord can be a powerful tool for the husband's salvation, when the **motive** is right. You can see how it might bring considerable pressure upon a rebellious man. For a wife to leave her husband because she is restless, dissatisfied or just hungry for a change would be unthinkable. The separation would be motivated out of selfishness and therefore evil.

> **OBSERVE:** Satan used the power of marital affection to separate Adam from God. In the separation showdown, the first man chose his wife over God. In the nutcracker technique, we reverse the process, using the separation showdown to bring a husband to the Lord. If the forces in marriage are mighty enough to make a man forsake his God, they must also be great enough to make a man consider his God. Eve was deceived, consequently her actions led her husband away from the Lord. But your actions will be insightful and can be used to lead your husband to the Lord. See the point? The fantastic forces in marriage can be used for good or evil. It's all in knowing how!

That we are correctly interpreting God's Word is seen by a closer look at the verse above. When Paul says, ". . . the wife should not **leave** her husband," that is a very strong word in the Greek. It is a legal term referring specifically to divorce. When he says, "IF SHE SHOULD DEPART," he obviously means for her to keep herself **available for reconciliation.** Hence Paul can only mean separation when he speaks of a wife leaving her husband.

WHEN THE MOTIVE IS RIGHT

That's what makes the difference in everything we do for Christ.

Marriage for marriage sake means nothing to God. What men view as successful marriages couldn't mean less to Him. He seeks to accomplish something through the marriage program. What? Preparing Christians to live with Him. That's the whole point of joining one man to one woman — for life. We are going to be joined to our One God — forever!

When two people are joined for life, the accumulated marital pressures are meant to CHANGE them. God counts on that. They learn to accommodate themselves to the differences in each other through self-denial and sacrifice. Personal ambitions are denied and set aside for the sake of each other. In bringing themselves to this selfless living, they become more and more like Jesus. If the goal of Christian marriage is preparation for the eternal marriage, then becoming more and more like Christ is the chief end of the marriage plan.

But what happens when a marriage does the opposite? When it defeats and frustrates God's intention instead of fulfilling it? What if two people begin to hate, rather than love each other? What if sacrifice and self-denial give way to viciousness and retaliation? What then? What is God's will when the earthly union of two souls **defeats His purpose** in their marriage?

Consider God's estimate of that marriage where the Christian wife is found changing **for the worse.** Where she becomes bitter, hard and vengeful thoughts fill her mind. Does it please God for such a thing to continue? Does He intend for the marriage to survive at the expense of the people? Does He desire that a marriage should stand even if the couple collapses inside that marriage? My firm answer is NO.

● Look what that would make God to be. At once He'd be a Lawyer, not a Father. He would appear more interested in legal technicalities of the Law than the plight of His people. Marriage is important, yea sacred and holy. But it is not that important to God. He will never sacrifice people for the sake of a program. Such a thing is contrary to all we know of His glorious nature. He loves people, not programs.

When a marriage begins to destroy the person it is supposed to build, it is time for another look, but **from God's point of view.** That's what can make a person's motive right. What did the Lord Jesus say when taken to task for plucking corn on the Sabbath? How did He answer? "The Sabbath was made for man, man was not made for the Sabbath!" (Mark 2:27). Those words apply here as well. "Marriage was made for man, man was not made for marriage!" Marriage exists for the sake of God's people, they do not exist for the sake of marriage. No minor distinction, that. Even so, I am not hinting at divorce. I speak only of one's motive in considering a separation.

Here, then, is the question to ask:

"Is my marriage situation making me bitter or better?"

BITTER OR BETTER?

Those words may sound alike, but they are worlds apart. Keep them in mind and they will provide the MOTIVE-KEY when separation becomes an approaching possibility.

If the situation in your home has been frictionizing for some time, a sizeable deposit of ill feeling smolders deep inside both of you. With all the pressure of step four coming upon your husband, his feelings could easily erupt. It should be no surprise when they do. But things haven't been so nice for you either. There've been times when you felt like saying something, but you didn't. You held your tongue, you suppressed your feelings. Yet those feelings didn't go too far away. They lurk just below the surface of your self-control.

If you have not yet learned to go to the Lord and dispose of your bitter feelings in heaven's waste basket, step four might bring you a surprise too. You could be astonished at the hellish, evil thoughts which linger in your mind. In an off-guarded moment, you may find yourself thinking about the day when that heathen you live with will get his "come uppins!" Oh, Satan is clever. His timing is seldom wrong.

Remember the Lord Jesus' warning . . . "WATCH and pray." Did not His instruction to WATCH come before His counsel to PRAY? And why, do you suppose? It is because Satan is able to plant ideas in our minds which can damage us even before we can get to our knees. He can introduce evil suggestions quicker than we can get to prayer. And when the marriage pot is boiling, he has an easy time of it. He has the power to stir thoughts and feelings inside a person before the victim knows it. Resentments and imagined retaliations occur in a flash, and should you let them linger for a few seconds you can be damaged.

DAMAGE. Every Christian should equip himself with a defense system for detecting and dealing with satanic activity. Satan has amazing powers, able to plant ideas in our minds which appear as our own. Who thinks to challenge an idea that arrives in his head as his own idea? No one, until he learns of the enemy who has the power to do this. Then it requires specific action on the part of the victim to resist Satan if he would be free of the awful impulses triggered by these thoughts. See the author's "Dealing With The Devil!" where a practical, four step plan for countering Satan's attack is offered.

● Marriage can damage a person. If your marriage is producing un-christlike thoughts and feelings in you, it could be dangerous. It is possible to receive spiritual injury within a marriage from which a Christian may never recover. And the real tragedy of it is one is forced to enter into heaven's marriage in that damaged condition. Watch, therefore. Look closely to see what your earthly marriage is doing to you. Is it preparing you to live with Jesus, or is it disqualifying you? How can it disqualify you? By turning you into a hostile, bitter person. You can pray all you like, but if living with an unsaved man under pearl/swine conditions is making you UNLIKE Jesus, you are slowly being destroyed by something God intended for your good.

A principle therefore emerges.

When a TEMPORARY earthly marriage situation begins to produce ETERNAL damage in a child of God, it is time to run. Don't walk, run.

A matter of priority

The eternal always has priority over that which is temporary. It is bad enough to be yoked to an unbeliever, but when that yoke begins to ruin you as an eternal partner of the Lord Jesus it is time to get out. Don't argue that marriage is good and therefore could never produce evil. There are many wonderful things in this life, which become deadly as they interfere with God's plan for a Christian's life. This might not be so if we didn't have an enemy who specializes in using good things for evil and vice versa.

Consider money. It is wonderful to have wealth and use it for Christ. But let it come between a man and his Lord and at once it is evil. Why, something as wonderful as the family bond can be dangerous. We've already noted what it did to Adam. He denied God for the sake of his wife. So with marriage, it is good and holy only so long as it fulfills the divine plan. Let it become the means for destroying one destined to be a marriage partner of the Lord Jesus, and it too becomes **an evil.** It is Satan's access and influence over our old natures that make it possible for him to use good things for evil purposes. When that happens it is time to flee. A person should put a marriage behind him as quickly as anything else that threatens his relationship with Christ.

● Think about the bitter Christian wife. Does she pray as she ought? Hardly. She's in no condition to talk to God. How can she with bitterness flooding her spirit? What does this do to her sweetness? It begins to fade. Is she then any longer a credit to her Master? Certainly not. Can fleshly feelings, satanically inspired, draw her closer to Christ? You know that's impossible. Is it then God's will for her to continue such a course? There's a way to find out for sure. We come to it now.

TO LEAVE OR NOT TO LEAVE?

That really is the question, isn't it? And one we cannot

answer glibly. Such a thing must be approached systematically, prayerfully and wisely. To be systematic, we must take
things in order:

1. **Ask God for wisdom.**

> **"If any of you lacks wisdom, let him ask of God, Who gives to
> all men generously and without reproach, and it will be given
> to him!"** (James 1:5).

This has to be first. God offers it, it's foolish not to take
advantage of it. Wisdom is not an increase in mental power.
It is the ability to SEE what God is doing in your life and
how His WORD bears on a particular situation. James assures
us God is eager to grant this ability.

2. **Study your marriage situation.**

That is, view your marriage in the light of what God reveals in His Word and see what it is doing to your maturity.
Is your marriage aiding or hindering your development in
the likeness of Christ. The KEY is what is happening to you
as a person. It doesn't take too much wisdom to SEE that
maturity in Christ means more to God than successful co-
existence with an unsaved man. If you cannot see this, then
surely there are other areas in your life where you have also
misunderstood the will of God.

Once you take the divine view of your marriage and conclude it is damaging your personality, you know a decision
has to be made. When waves of ungodly feelings sweep your
spirit, when hateful and vengeful notions are tolerated in
your mind, you know you can't wait much longer. If you see
yourself becoming BITTER, rather than SWEETER . . . you
must make a decision.

3. **You decide to leave.**

Your insight to the marriage program, your right handling
of God's Word and your ability to see what is happening to
you . . . bring you to this conclusion. So you make the necessary decision. It's painful, you come to it slowly and prayerfully. But finally you reach the settled conviction . . . a

separation is needed. Yet, there is something you have to do about this decision BEFORE you put it into operation. It has to be tested. How?

 Present the decision to God for His approval or disapproval.

How is that done? Here is another wonderful principle from the Word of God:

"Let the peace of God RULE in your hearts . . ." (Col. 3:15).

Before I explain what I mean by that, first we must distinguish between the peace OF GOD and peace WITH GOD. Peace **with** God has to do with the hostility between God and the unsaved. The wrath of God abides on those outside of Christ (John 3:36). But when a soul turns to Jesus, that wrath is removed and peace is declared. The new convert experiences a peace in his soul such as when a war ends. And indeed his war with God is over. But that is not the peace involved in your decision.

 The PEACE OF GOD is that inner tranquility a Christian may know even as the storms of life beat against him. It is a sereneness of spirit which says, **"My life is in God's hands, and nothing can hurt me as long as I am in the center of His will. No matter what situation developes, I have the assurance God is arranging what is best for me!"** This is a peace which has to do with being in the **will of God.** It is the same peace the Lord Jesus displayed when He walked so stately and nonplussed through the Gospels. No money in His pockets, no place to lay His head, scorned by crowds yet no fear gripped Him for He was at rest in His Father's will.

This same peace is our inheritance from Jesus. He gave it to us.* The only thing that can upset it, is getting out of the Father's will. Consequently it provides us with a wonderful way of knowing when we are in the will of God.

---

*John 14:27

123

● Peace is a FEELING. People FEEL either peaceful or upset. And God grants this feeling as an INDICATOR of His will. That's why it can exercise RULE or DOMINION over our hearts. That's what makes it a dependable guide. So what did Paul counsel when an unbelieving one departs? **"Let him (or her)!"** And why? Look . . . **"For God has called us to peace"** (1 Cor. 7:15b). Of course you feel restless while you struggle with your decision. There is agony in giving birth to decisions. But that's not the point. It's what you feel **after** you PRESENT YOUR DECISION TO GOD. He is responsible to let you know His will . . . and He does.

Here's how it is done. You commit your decision to God in prayer. Even as you do, you are ready to perform His will either way. It is simply a matter of WHAT HE WANTS. Then you wait. Check your spirit an hour later. How do you feel about the decision? Do it again the next day. Do wild, stabbing, seizures of unrest grab you? Does your spirit toss day and night? Or do you have the settled assurance that no matter how unpleasant it may be, it simply has to be done?

Don't confuse uneasiness about your future with God's witness to your spirit. Isolate, if you can, your concerns for your personal welfare. Focus on your decision and how you feel as you think of living for Jesus. It's how you feel **about that decision** that counts, not how you feel about your problems. Your outward circumstances may be awful, but you can still feel right about the change. That's what is important. What really concerns you is, **"How does God feel about my decision?"** When He communicates His feelings to you . . . you can FEEL THEM. But don't mix them with concern over your welfare.

> **NOTE:** Satan can mask God's communications by stirring up WORRY within you. When this happens you must deal with him first to clear the air, so that worry-feelings do not confound the witness of God. Dealing with Satan in such things is no slight matter. Neither is it something for speculation. It is something you have to do. Satan will never let you alone until you resist him in the power of Jesus' Name. James tells us to do this in no uncertain language . . . "Resist the devil and he will flee from you" (Ja. 4:7). I tell you if you don't, it will be very hard to separate the witness of God from these worry feelings Satan arouses in your spirit.

● But someone says, **"I don't feel anything!"** All right, in that case you have nothing to fear. God has left the matter entirely in your hands. It is not uncommon for Him to do this. You can be sure if you were in danger, He'd let you know. Sometimes our God, being so great, can take your decision . . . **whichever way you decide** . . . and make it work out for your best interest. Only One with His genius could do such a thing. So whenever there is a lack of assurance from heaven, don't be concerned. All that is ever necessary to be in the center of God's will, is the compelling desire to be there. God takes it from there. He is faithful to warn when you are about to step out of His will. Honestly, there is no way to miss. That is one of the thrills in living for Christ!

This absence of any indication from heaven is really peace. You may not recognize it as that, but it is peace, nonetheless. Your spirit is unmoved within you, indicating you **are not** out of the will of God. That's what is important. Whenever a Christian is out of God's will, there is no peace. He cannot allow any child to feel peaceful about a decision contrary to His will, such a thing would violate the office of the Holy Spirit. **"For God has called us to peace."**

Paul was not merely being pious when he added those words to the verse above. God has not called us to hatred or strife. The words of the Apostle have the force of, **"The Christian is not called to remain with a heathen consort where doing so interferes with his peaceful balance in God's presence."** To make someone endure a situation that destroyed his peaceful progress in Christ, would be contrary to the Christian call. Paul's following words confirm this:

> "For how do you know, O wife, whether you will save your husband? Or how do you know, O husband, whether you will save your wife?" . . . [by remaining in that situation] (1 Cor. 7:16).

● Paul is telling the Christian NOT to remain in a situation that violates the PEACE of GOD. There is no assurance a partner will be saved by perpetuating such an arrangement. To the contrary, he is offering this as **grounds** for SEPARATION. The Christian's peace is not to be marred, for something as unlikely as converting an unbelieving man **by living with him.** Paul appears to be answering the argument, "Wouldn't a man's chances of being saved be forfeited should his wife leave?" The reply is **no** . . . not if the wife remains unmarried and is available for reconciliation as soon as her heathen husband is reconciled to God. All the husband has to do to be re-joined to his wife is to be joined to God.

 5.   Do it . . . leave!

After checking your spirit for God's witness and finding His PEACE indication, go. Carry out your decision. And do it heartily as unto the Lord with a view to your husband's salvation.

> **WARNING:** Don't think to use this device as an escape from an unpleasant marriage. It won't work. God alone can grant the witness you need to your heart, and it will not come unless your decision is in His will. He will not sanction a separation merely because the road is hard and you are suffering. You can expect His witness only when remaining in the marriage situation will result in eternal damage to your person and injure your relationship with Him.

BEFORE YOU GO

When it comes time to discuss the separation with your husband, give no hint of the plans you have already made. Bring up the whole idea of separation as a possibility only . . .

> "What would you think, John, if we separated for a time? Perhaps we need time away from each other to think about our marriage and see if it is worth salvaging. I know the Lord's presence in my life disturbs you awfully. And lately it has caused so much trouble between us. Wouldn't it be a good idea to separate and see what our marriage looks like when we let the emotional fires die down?"

Your remark is calculated to sample his reaction **to the idea** of separation. A few words from him will tell what you are up against in leaving. If he goes into a rage, or behaves emo-

126

tionally, then discount what he says. He won't mean his words. A few days later his statements will be nearer the truth. The more the fires in him can settle down, the more objectively you can discuss a separation. It might be a few days are needed for him to get over the shock of your question. Even though you bring it up as a possibility only. And you might need a day or two to compose yourself. There is no hurry and you are moving according to plan.

> **CAUTION:** Do not tell him you are leaving. Don't make such a statement flat out. When you raise the matter it is for consideration only. You want to take his pulse and see what further planning is needed on the basis of his reaction. When you are finally ready to leave, say nothing. Just up and go. Your plans have been made, simply carry them out. It could be a mistake, a serious one, if you reveal your plans to your husband. If he interferes it will add to your burden.

Leave a note.

Make it sweet. Even though you must clench your fist and grit your teeth to put kindness on paper, do it. You must

If you have to go——GO!

give the Holy Spirit something He can use, so let your words on paper be of a wooing nature. You want this man saved. And since no one can argue with a piece of paper, you write your goodbye instead of saying it. Besides, it allows you to **choose** your words with deliberate care. This is something you cannot do in the middle of an emotional scene. It could go like this:

> "Dear John, I think it would be better for both of us if I leave for a time. We need a chance to review our marriage and weigh the prospect and reasons for continuing to live together. I thank you for the years you have shared with me, some have been really wonderful. I will miss you. But I will also pray for you. Oh that the Lord Jesus would be able to come into your heart and life and really make us one.
>
> Lovingly,
>
> Signed...

Does that take courage? Yes, a lot of it. And power in the Holy Spirit if feelings of resentment have been running high. It takes supernatural strength to dethrone your ego and say kind words to an embittered, abusive mate, at the same time holding out the hint of reunion. But you can also see what the Spirit of God might do with such an act of humility and self-denial. There is power in being clay. Miracles occur when we submit ourselves to HIM like this!

So there you are. Those are the five steps you can take and remain in the center of the Lord's will as you give a final squeeze on the nutcracker.

That last squeeze.

Can you see now that leaving your husband is a WORK? The note you left for him is your LIGHT. The Spirit of God uses the combination to give the final squeeze of the nutcracker. This is the last resort, the most crushing move a wife can make. No other action has the force of this one.

But it is not easy for a woman to leave her husband and provider. It is not a decision one reaches suddenly and without pain and stress of soul. But like the trip to the dentist, it finally becomes necessary. You have but one life in which to prepare yourself for Jesus and the heavenly wedding. The earthly rehearsal must not be allowed to mar it. When that showdown with your unsaved mate occurs, the Lord Jesus will have to mean more to you than any comforts or security.

As an actress you may feel terrible walking out on the show. But there is one time in the theater when the players are justified in quitting — when the play itself is so bad it threatens the careers of the actors. No one can afford to stay in such a play. It's not pleasant, no actress wants to do this, but one's future has to be considered. It's just not worth it to end a career by remaining in a bad play.

Similarly, to allow ETERNAL DAMAGE to occur to you through remaining in a ruinous marriage can also be wrong. Particularly if it is within your power to do something about it. Even more so when you know you can make such moves and remain fully in the center of God's will. Bear in mind we have not even hinted at divorce or re-marriage. Only separation is under discussion here, and then as a healthy last squeeze on the nutcracker. You are ready to be united with this man, but only in Christ. Your purpose and motive is his salvation. If that does not occur, I have not counseled you to seek a divorce. I will say, however, that a life lived alone is better than one spent inside a fatal marriage.

WILL HE COME BEGGING?

Your husband, like yourself, is a freewill agent. He will do exactly as he pleases. Will he come to you with pleas for you to return to him? He might. If the final squeeze is enough to crack his shell, there's no doubt about it. He will come. When he has had time to review the wonderful privilege of living with a sweet, Christian woman, the marriage will look pretty good to him. When he recalls how gently and carefully she served him, the squeeze will get worse. When he recalls that lovely home she made for him and the faithful way she met his needs, particularly his sexual needs, he'll begin to discount his reasons for rebellion. Christ can't be that bad. When he comes, be ready for his . . .

"What do you want me to do?"

Praise the Lord! This is what you have been waiting for! You'll have to be ready with a specific, clear cut answer. We'll deal with that in the next chapter which tells precisely what to do when that shell cracks. We have something else to consider now.

Husbands are tricky. Watch out!

Sometimes they will promise anything to get their wives back. They even think they mean it. But you don't want him coming around **just to get you back.** You've gone too far and suffered too much. You don't want to go through it again. So — even if he promises to **consider** Christianity, even to give it **a try** . . . DO NOT RETURN TO HIM. You must have **more than promises.** It would be better for you to remain separated from him for the rest of your life, than return to that damaging situation.

The reason you left the home in the first place, was **not** because you didn't like being married or your mate. You left for the sake of the Lord Jesus and your eternal relationship to HIM. That must also be the **basis for your return.** SO DON'T ACCEPT PROMISES.

 Before you take him back, your husband must be CONFRONTED with the PERSON of Christ so that he might DO SOMETHING WITH JESUS one way or the other. And you must be present to see it. From now on, your relationship with this man has to be based on WHAT HE DOES with Christ. Everything changes once you leave that house, or he does, whichever the case

may be. Do not let yourself be deceived. Make no commitment or attempt any reunion with this man until his relationship with Christ is settled. If you do, you'll only open the door for more agony and suffering, and may end up like some, who go through repeated separations.

Once you put this heathen from you, you must not yoke yourself to him again until he **receives** Christ. If you do, it will be a deliberate action against the will of the Lord. You will be joining yourself to an unclean man . . . and it doesn't matter that you once dwelt with him. The point is, you are now free. You should look upon your return to him as seriously as if you were again marrying an unsaved man. So don't, I repeat, don't go back on the basis of promises. You are in the same position as a young girl considering marriage to a man who MIGHT be saved after they are married, because he promises to go to church with her.

If your separation becomes permanent through your husband's refusal to receive Christ, then let it be. It costs something to be a disciple of Jesus Christ. At no point have I minimized the cost in reaching your mate for Christ. If you win him, you won't mind. If you don't, be assured that the Lord Jesus will more than compensate for anything He takes from you. You'll never be sorry if you put Christ first!

NOW HERE'S A LADY

Mrs. D------- had separation in mind when she arrived at my study. Her husband was treating her like dirt. He squandered the weekly income, buying high-powered sports cars awkward for family use. He had a fondness for a friend across the street, spending long hours there playing cards. His friend's wife made no bones about her crush on Mrs. D's husband. And he liked that.

The list of his excesses and abuses totaled a miserable bondage for Mrs. D. He scoffed at her religion, calling her a fanatic. He handled the money, allowing her but a pittance for herself. She was his maid. He informed her she was well off to have a roof over her head. The kids were hers, he said, she could take care of them. He wasn't mean about it, and never did he hit her. He just failed to grow up.

"Do you hate your husband?" I asked.

"No. Down inside he's not a bad man. He doesn't mean to be so self-centered. It's as though he can't help himself."

"Do you have any love for him?"

"In a way I suppose I do. But he has no idea what he is doing to me. I'm not sure I can go on like this much longer."

Her words confirmed what I suspected. Besides, others had refused to be silent about this woman's suffering. They filled me in on the details. Though all felt sorry for her, they agreed her suffering was turning her into a beautiful Christian.

No question about her soul-pain, she had plenty. But she was not returning evil for evil. Resentments did not accumulate within her. Instead, she was becoming patient and gentle under the testings. Her spirit was tender, compassionate, she learned to forgive "seventy times seven." Her marriage was producing in her exactly what God longed to see in all His children. It was doing precisely what God intends for every Christian marriage. Only in her case, the process was speeded by the more intense marital pressures. And so intense were they, no one would have blamed her had she left her husband.

She wanted to know what to do. Should she leave this man or not? I didn't answer directly but laid before her the divine purpose in marriage. Recognition came to her face when she saw that marriage is supposed to be a pressure pot. She identified with that hard fact quickly. She began to relax as she saw how God's will was being accomplished in her. She was a dedicated person, so being in the will of God meant more to her than all of her distresses. Her mind was made up even before I got the words out.

● Separation was out. She couldn't leave this man. It would be wrong to leave. Her marriage was a spiritual gold mine, from God's point of view. She was getting rich in Christ, more prepared for the heavenly wedding with each passing day. As long as she was turning into the likeness of Jesus, separation was out of the question. Her biggest thrill came upon learning of the nutcracker technique.

Her real problem, you see, was not whether to leave . . . but WHAT TO DO. As soon as she saw **the plan,** she confessed it was not so much the suffering that bothered her, but the lack of knowing what to do about it. When she learned it could all be used in the power of the Spirit for the salvation of her husband, she was overjoyed.

I handed her a piece of paper and a pen. Then recited two verses for her. She already knew them, but I had her write them down as ammunition for what lie ahead.

> **"There hath no temptation taken you but such as is common to man: but God, Who is faithful, will not suffer you to be tempted beyond that which ye are able, but will with the temptation also make a way of escape that ye may be able to bear it"** (1 Cor. 10:13).

and . . .

> **". . . My grace is sufficient for thee: for my strength is made perfect in weakness. Most gladly therefore will I glory in my infirmities that the power of Christ may rest on me"** (2 Cor. 12:9).

A zealous Christian woman, she warmed enthusiastically to the keeping power of God's Word. She accepted these verses as God's guarantees, trusting Him to sustain her while she went to work with the nutcracker. She was eager to give it a try.

You should have seen her when she left my study. Was she ever alive! I suspect the dear lady could hardly wait to get home and begin working with the Holy Spirit. She was cheered by a definite plan which might salvage her husband for Christ. She was thrilled over step-by-step know-how which could exploit every bit of her suffering and use it to "squeeze" her husband. How many women, do you suppose, suffer for the lack of similar counsel? Multitudes, I'd say. May God use the insights of this book to bring Mrs. D's comfort to each of them.

SUMMARY

This chapter contains a startling idea — the matter of leaving a man with God's sanction. The earthly marriage program is so biblical and basic to life as we know it, it seems almost sacrilegious to hint such a thing. Yet the Apostle Paul goes beyond hinting when he says . . .

"But **IF SHE DEPARTS,** let her remain unmarried . . ." (1 Cor. 7:11a).

Let's go over the steps leading to a separation decision.

1. Ask God for wisdom. This is so that you may SEE how your marriage appears in His sight. Your view shifts to the divine side, rather than the human. Spiritual vision is necessary now since there are no external clues for those who remove themselves from the **letter of the law.** You are now to be guided by the Spirit.

2. Survey your marriage with a view to SEEING what it is doing to you as a forthcoming marriage partner of the Lord Jesus.

Marriage is a drama, instituted by God and therefore sacred and solemn. Nonetheless it is but earthly preparation for the marriage of the Lamb. It is in the light of its temporariness that you consider what it is doing to your personality.

3. Make your decision. Don't argue the pros and cons any longer, it only prolongs the suffering. Check carefully to see if you are being spiritually hurt and if you are, make the decision to leave. But don't do anything **about** the decision until you get God's OK on it. At least give Him a chance to disapprove it, if that is His pleasure.

4. Present your decision to God in prayer. Ask Him if it is OK. Don't rehash the matter with Him, He's already been through it with you. As you bring your decision to Him, **remain consenting to do His will** no matter what. The chances are your decision is His will, for the wisdom granted in step one usually shows things as they are. If your decision is contrary to His will, He will definitely let you know.

5. Leave. Having tested your decision in God's presence, owning the settled assurance you are not out of His will . . . get ready to leave. Do not announce your plans. Make all arrangements before saying anything to your husband. Know where you are going. Arrange for your finances. If

you are in the will of God, you can count on Him to open doors for you and prepare the way.

NO DIVORCE

Again, we are **not** talking about divorce here, only SEPA-RATION from a heathen husband to whom one is UNEQUAL-LY YOKED. And even the separation has RECONCILIATION in view. The separation idea is not mine, but that of the Apostle Paul. Since it is in the Word of God, I have taken the liberty of using it for the final squeeze of the nutcracker.

> **NOTE: If you are interested in the author's approach to divorce and re-marriage, you can secure a copy of "The Compassionate Side of Divorce." There the matter is dealt with compassion-ately with consideration for the casualties of the marriage pro-gram. It does not present the legalistic, traditional point of view.**

We come now to the pay off of this technique. That sweet moment when your bewildered husband says, "Tell me what to do, Honey. I'll do anything, I'll be anything. Just tell me how." What joy! His resistance is now gone. He's ready to meet Jesus. And he does . . . next.

Chapter Eight

WHEN THE SHELL CRACKS!

Know what metal salvage people do with old wrecked cars? They squeeze them. They use a pressure so great it crumples a steel automobile into a wad. Now you've been applying great pressure also. Not the kind that collapses cars, but that which crumbles the resistance of an unsaved husband.

You've joined forces with the Holy Spirit, applying increasing pressure on your mate. You can hardly wait for that shell to break, exposing the man inside to Jesus. Like your Lord, you hate the status quo. You are determined not to let years go by waiting for it to happen. That's why you have been using the nutcracker technique. If you are married to a man with whom you should NOT BE LIVING, let's find out as fast as possible. Why waste years, when some squeezing can settle the matter. In a few weeks, perhaps.

SIMPLE, BUT NOT EASY

It doesn't take much to use a nutcracker. However, the tougher the shell, the harder you have to squeeze. And the harder you squeeze, the rougher it is on you. I have not deceived you with the thought this plan was easy. It takes the closest cooperation with the Holy Spirit, an utter dependence on His supernatural working. It is in His power that you bridle your tongue, maintaining sweet Christian composure. It is so easy to REACT when a formidable husband takes advantage and abuses you. Amazing grace is needed for playing your part. The success of this plan depends on your behaving as **a Spirit-filled** actress.

Acting is not easy. This part is difficult.

You can see that it is only by the strictest discipline of yourself that you can do this role. It is your sweet posture that puts the squeeze on your mate. It will drive you to prayer. Your pillow will soak tears which only Jesus can wipe away. But it is worth it. Your husband's salvation is no slight matter. Of all the mission fields on this globe, your home is the one charged to you. You may give to missions and pray for the lost, but if you abandon that soul who shares your bed—shame on you. And don't think to say, "He isn't going to be my husband in heaven, so why bother?" Of all the people in the world to bother with, he is the one. It would be better for you to neglect the "ninety and nine" in the world, than this one under your own roof.

Even if your husband turns out to be a hardened enemy of Jesus, you won't be sorry for the trouble it takes to find it out. Your most valuable possession is time. You have but one span of years in which to get ready for the life to come. Planned action lets you salvage years which might otherwise be wasted. So what is a little pain?

YOUR HUSBAND IS SAVED!

When does it happen? Each case is sure to be different. Somewhere along the scale of increasing pressures, your mate yields. Maybe it is the very day you begin to let your light shine. Or, if he is stubborn, it could take six months. Perhaps you had to go as far as leaving the house for a time. It really doesn't matter just where in the plan salvation comes to your husband. The joy is, he finally comes to Christ.

How does it happen? Probably in one of three ways:

1. THE GO TO CHURCH METHOD

It is not uncommon, once the shell cracks, for an unsaved husband to venture cautiously, **"It might be nice if we went to church as a family."** You can expect him to back that with some face-saving remark such as, **"If it means that much to you, I might as well go and find out what it's all about."** Don't mistake this touch of humor for a lack of seriousness. Inside he's serious . . . perhaps scared.

● The male ego is funny. You, a woman, have brought about your mate's surrender. You can expect his maleish pride to raise its head clothed with humor. He might come out with, "If you can't lick 'em, you might as well join 'em." At this stage he no doubt pictures Christianity as church-going. Later he will learn that it is an **experience** with Christ — a new birth. Don't bother to straighten him out on that. Let him think what he will. When he is face to face with Jesus — IN PERSON — the truth will be clear enough.

So he accompanies you to church. Accept that as God's working. If your church gives an invitation to go forward and receive Christ, take advantage of it. As heads are bowed in prayer, the music playing, lean over and whisper:

"Come on, Honey. I'll go with you." If he hesitates, press slightly, **"There's nothing to be afraid of. I'll be with you. Come on."**

Should he refuse, give no outward indication of disappointment or displeasure. If you must say something, make it . . . **"Maybe next time it will be easier."**

> **CAUTION:** While the "go to church" method is perhaps the most common, it is not always the safest. If your pastor is truly sharp and knows how to present Christ ALIVE and in Person, that is one thing. If he is vague and uses symbolic talk, it can be deadly. Your husband must MEET Christ and RECEIVE Him. If you have the slightest doubt of your pastor's ability to accomplish this, seek another person who can. Generally you don't have this problem in vigorous evangelical churches, but in traditional churches you must be very careful.

2. THE PROFESSIONAL SOUL-WINNER

I call him that, not because money is involved, but because he makes it his **business** to be skilled in handling souls and presenting Christ **alive.** And it is a skill. He can be called a **personal evangelist.** You find such people ministering in jails, hospitals, bus depots, crusades. They are sometimes called altar workers. Usually one or two can be found in every evangelical church. They are business-like, because they have a burden for lost souls and have equipped themselves to reach people at the PERSONAL LEVEL.

CAUTION: Do not take for granted that an exciting preacher is also a skilled soul-winner. Some are wonderfully gifted for mass level communications, but entirely lacking in the skill of personal confrontation with Christ. A cleverly worded pulpit invitation is a far different thing from introducing Jesus to someone in person. Pulpit invitations can be ignored, but Christ standing BEFORE YOU . . . waiting to enter your heart . . . CANNOT. One may hear that Jesus is waiting to save him, but FACING HIM, required to DO SOMETHING about Him, is an experience. Pulpit oratory must never be confused with this personal skill. Not every preacher has both.

Well, your husband went to church with you. But he didn't go forward on the invitation. So you decide to arrange for someone to come by the house and deal with him privately. How do you go about it? Quite simply. Since he has made his first trip to the church, a follow-up call would be perfectly in order. He probably expects a visitor from the church anyway, most people do. And you know he will, if you plant the suggestion in his mind . . .

"I'm sure someone will be calling from the church. It's customary after a person has visited, to make a call on him. It's a matter of courtesy."

That paves the way for a **personal worker** to call. You make sure it isn't an ordinary church-volunteer, but someone skilled in winning souls. If he belongs to your church, so much the better.

Here's what you can expect to see.

The visitor arrives from the church. The conversation opens with mention of your husband's first visit. But the worker doesn't spend much time with that, he wants to ease into his soul-winning plan. After acknowledging your husband's visit, he shifts to relaxing topics:

1. He inquires about the family. How many children? Names? Schools, etc.

HINT: Let your husband answer these questions, if he will. True, they are of the kind to which wives respond the quickest, but you want your mate to involve himself in the conversation. See him relax as he chats about matters which are familiar to him.

2. Your husband's job is mentioned next. He talks freely about that. If you interrupt, make it something like . . . **"Tell him what you do at work, dear."** That way your insight helps the conversation along.

3. Then your visitor asks HOW (not if) your husband enjoyed his first visit to the church. Actually, the soul-winner uses this as a device to begin taking your husband's spiritual measurements. The answer tells him a lot. Be sure you do not answer this FOR your husband. Some wives eagerly rush in with answers leaving their husbands sitting there silently. Don't you be guilty of this.

4. Then your visitor comes out with the reason he has called, his mission. You may smile when you see him do this, because you know what is coming. He employs a key phrase which makes it natural for a soul-winning interview to begin. The reason I am alerting you to it now, is that you will show no surprise or say anything to interrupt the procedure.

● I have outlined the FOUR STEPS to give you an idea how the visit will be conducted. If you know what to expect, you can cooperate with the worker. Just keep four letters in mind . . .

F-O-R-M*

and you will have the format for the visit. Those letters spell out the flow of the conversation: F (family), O (occupation), R (religious interest), M (mission or message).

---

*This is the conversation control device as found in the author's book, "Visitation Made Easy." This manual sets forth the skill of approaching a house, getting inside, and completing a successful visit at the caller-centered; church-centered; or Christ-centered levels. If you wish to learn how to execute an effective visit to a home in 20 minutes, you'll want this practical book.

NOTE: Don't give yourself away should you see the conversation going almost word for word as I have told you. At the same time don't think to credit me with prophetic insight. This is the FORM method of visitation in wide use among evangelical churches today.

The soul-winner is ready to close in on your husband.

> **"By any chance did you happen to get one of our church calendars when you visited Sunday?"**

> "No, I don't believe I did. Did we get one Honey?" (You know he didn't, so does the visitor. This is merely part of the technique.)

> **"Here, let me give you one."**

● Watch the visitor's hand. Upon those words he reaches into his pocket. Out comes a small card, obviously the calendar. He rises from his chair and walks toward your husband. He holds out the card, offering it to your mate. This action puts the worker beside your husband, in a position to begin his soul-winning plan. Right here I will let you in on a few words of the dialogue. It helps to know what is coming.

The soul-winner starts his plan.

> **"This is not an ordinary calendar. On the other side is a picture that has puzzled Christians for a long time. (Pause. The card is turned over.) There is something missing, isn't there?"**

> NOTE: See what is happening? Your husband receives the card calendar side up. That's disarming. Like everyone else, he naturally turns it over. Ah, on the back side is a painting of Christ at the Door. That question from the worker causes his eyes to scan the picture in search for what is missing. Behold the power of this: (1) Your husband's ego has been challenged. Everything else is swept from his mind as he tries to locate the missing item. (2) Unconsciously he is examining a religious scene. A visual representation of Christ is in his hand. Nothing has been said to indicate a soul-winning interview was under way . . . BUT IT IS!

"Before I tell you what is missing, and so that I don't trespass your feelings in any way, perhaps I should first ask whether or not you have any interest in spiritual things?" (Pause.)

NOTE: Those familiar with the author's "Soul Winning Made Easy," will recognize this as the #1 approach question of the X-RAY technique. There is no Testament in sight. This is very casual, conversational. The worker is extremely polite. Moving easily, in no way appearing to intrude. He shows the greatest respect for your husband's feelings. But don't discount his nonchalance. His moves are calculated with the precision of a fine watch. Your husband is going to face Christ in a few minutes, nothing short of a divine interruption can prevent it.

 You watch. It is fascinating to behold. The spiritual subtlety is remarkable. The worker is moving very casually from step to step. You hardly notice when he brings out the Testament, his eyes never leave your husband's face. You sense the supernatural occurring. Your soul begins to talk to the Holy Spirit. You study your husband's face. The Spirit is working, you can see it! You read God's power in the eyes and nods of your husband's head. You unconsciously nod your head in agreement as the truth rolls from the worker's lips.

HINT: Those nods of your head are a terrific asset to the worker. Your husband continually wonders what you think of all this. He feels safer if he can see your nodded approval to what is happening. It assures him that this is what you have been wanting for him all along. Be sure to nod when the worker says, "We're all sinners," or "the gift is in Christ," or "We must receive Christ." It helps the worker more than you can realize. So your part is vital too.

Then comes the close. The visitor presses for the decision . . .

"Jesus is waiting to come into your heart, right now. Will you open the door? Will you let Him in?"

NOTE: Be ready for your husband's searching glance at this point. He is pressed to act, to DO SOMETHING with Christ. He will look your way for a final indication. His eyes will be saying, "Is this what I am supposed to do?" The Spirit is saying yes, but you nod your approval too. It aids his total surrender.

● Your husband's head goes down. Your heart shouts inside you as you hear the words of prayer. Aloud he asks Jesus to come into his heart and be his personal Saviour. It's over. Now you can do anything you like — cry — dance — shout, but most of all, thank the wonderful Lord for the miracle you've just seen. The Holy Spirit has won your husband. Walk over and embrace your new **Christian** mate!

3. THE DO IT YOURSELF METHOD

This is the one I prefer. Some wives, though, are reluctant to lead their own husbands to Christ. They don't feel qualified, or they feel it is not their place. The truth is, they are without doubt the very best ones. Why? Usually a man and a wife are alone when his surrender comes out . . .

"All right Dear. I give up . . . what do you want me to do?"

That is the golden moment. What will you do? Wring your hands in despair, agonizing . . . **"Oh, if only so and so were here!"** Dear wife, if you are prepared, you can lead your husband to Jesus in five minutes, and very easily too. If you are not, it means you have to make hurried arrangements for someone else to do it. What will Satan be doing during that time?

 As soon as those words come from your husband's lips, the alarm goes off in Satan's headquarters. He's about to lose one of his subjects. His staff springs to action. Machinery is set in motion, calculated to hinder your husband's surrender. There will never be a better time than right now. And Satan knows it.

SO BE READY

There is no reason why you can't be ready for that moment. It doesn't matter what exact words come from your husband. The surrender is always the same, even if the words come out like this:

"Well, being a Christian couldn't be any worse than what I am going through now. I'm certainly not happy the way I am. I might as well give in and get it over with."

That's it. Move! Satan already has. Reach over, take the phone off the hook. That can block one of his favorite interruptions. Don't worry about missing any calls. The Holy Spirit takes care of all such details as that. Silently ask God to hold Satan off for a few minutes.

"But I'm no soul-winner!" You say.

"I know you're not. But how nice it would be if you were."

HINT: Should the Holy Spirit providentially arrange for soul-winning training to be offered at your church while you are using the nutcracker technique, be sure to get in on it. Such training intensifies your confidence. We can't count on such a thing, but I mention it in case it happens to be in the Spirit's plan. This "Do-it-yourself" step assumes you are NOT a trained soul-winner.

 In your purse you have placed something in anticipation of this moment. It is a tool you will use to lead your husband to Christ. It requires NO TRAINING to use it. I am giving you now all the know-how you need for using this tool to confront your husband with Christ. The name of it is . . . **"Your Biggest Decision."** When you read the dialogue below, you'll see how easy it is to use.

ACTION

"Come here dear and sit down beside me."

From your purse you draw out your copy of **"Your Biggest Decision."** Hold it in front of him. It is not open, yet.

"What I want you to do is explained right here. This booklet tells what is involved in becoming a Christian. It tells exactly HOW to be one. We're going to read it together."

NOTE: "Your Biggest Decision" is a 15¢ booklet. It sets forth the mechanics of receiving Christ step by step. The plan in it is identical to the one found in "Soul-Winning Made Easy." The difference here is, the one using the plan is NOT a trained soul-winner. It is designed to be read, so that a man can receive Christ **by reading it.** Putting it another way, a man can lead himself to Christ with this tool. The decision it secures is just as valid as the one secured by a personal worker. It is ideal for those times when a soul-winning interview is not possible, such as we have before us now.

"I'm going to read the words aloud, but I want you to read them too. In fact, some of the lines I want you to read instead of my reading them. We can stop anywhere to discuss something that isn't clear to you."

HINT: You stop only to clear up something he doesn't seem to understand. Satan is working on your husband's thought-processes, so avoid every non-related question he raises. Simply defer it by saying, "That's a good question dear. I'll answer it in a bit, but let's move on." With Satan on your trail, you don't dare allow any long pauses. As soon as your husband understands move right on.

● When you reach page 21, where it asks . . . "The Lord Jesus is waiting to come into your heart, right now. Will you open the door?" Use your finger to point to the words on the page. Turn to your husband and ask . . .

"What does that say there?"

"Yes I will." He is just reading words now.

NOTE: These words on his lips condition him for prayer. They tend to pre-dispose him to speak to the Lord Jesus, which he will be doing shorty. Now look again at the page. See where it says . . . "Get to a place where you can be alone?" Find it? Good. Substitute the word "We," for "you," so that it now reads . . . "Get to a place where WE can be alone." And do the same again in the line below, so that it reads . . . "We're alone now." Then continue reading until you come to the prayer. Your husband should read that aloud. Ask him to.

"Dear, these are the very words a person says to Jesus in prayer when he is ready to become a Christian. It is talking to Jesus just

145

like this and meaning it, that makes a person a Christian. A second ago you read the words, "Yes I will." Could you now say them to Jesus—and mean them?"

"Yes."

"All right, then you read that prayer out loud?"

● He does. So far it has been a matter of reading only. He has not yet spoken personally to the Lord. To get him to do that, I must ask you to do something that is not written on the pages of your booklet. Here is what to say to him:

"Now dear, I want you to bow your head with me. I am going to pray, using the same words you just read. But I am going to say them in short phrases. I want you to say them after me. But don't speak them to me. Picture the Lord Jesus as standing here before you, waiting to come into your heart. Say them to Him. He is waiting to hear them from you."

HINT: Do not wait for his reply to your statement. Let your hand go to his shoulder and rest there firmly. Bow your head without looking at him, ignoring anything he might do. Ah . . . feel that? Movement in his shoulder indicates he has dropped his head too. That bowed head, dear wife, tells you his surrender has taken place. He is ready to speak to Jesus. Then you begin . . .

"Dear Lord Jesus . . . I confess that I am a sinner . . . I need your forgiveness . . . and I want your life for my own. I give you mine . . . for what it is worth. I here and now . . . open my heart to Thee . . . I now put my trust . . . in you as my personal Savior. Amen."

"Oh, darling, that's wonderful!" (But you control your feelings. Be ready to move on.) **"But let's read the rest before we stop."**

● The reading is finished. The praying is over. Close the booklet. Look your husband squarely in the eye and ask . . .

"Did you really mean that Dear? As far as you are concerned, have you really opened your heart to Christ. If you have honestly and truly opened your heart to the Lord Jesus . . . and feel it is open to Him this second . . . would you reach over and squeeze my hand?"

146

He does! The joy of the Lord floods your being! It's over!

Why do you think I had you ask your husband for that squeeze? Can you guess? For weeks now you have been putting the squeeze on him. Now he has just squeezed you. What a wonderful squeeze. It tells you that the glory of a Christian home awaits you both!

IT'S WORTH IT!

There you have it, the entire NUTCRACKER TECHNIQUE from start to finish. You can see that I had to assume your husband to be a stubborn man, resisting the Gospel all the way — even to the point of separation. That gives you the over-view of the whole plan. However, your real husband may require very little pressure, just a slight squeeze.

● But be assured of this: the moment you try this plan in fellowship with the Spirit, a door of adventure opens. Just a few squeezes can convince you of that. If you will set aside a few minutes each day for intimacy with Jesus, so that together you might fulfill the task of reaching your mate, a new glory will fill your being. There is nothing to match the excitement of moving in the power of God!

So don't let the prospect of a little pain keep you from the blessing which beckons. Consider childbirth. Does the mere fact of a little pain keep women from having children? Indeed not. They want their babies, pain or no pain. And as soon as they have them, the pain is quickly forgotten. So it is with this plan. When it is all over and he's saved, who remembers the pain?

If you think it is worth some pain to have children, then you ought to agree it is worth the pain it takes to have a Christian home. Everything worthwhile has its price. What would you pay to be one in Christ with your husband? Yes, there's a little pain in this process . . .

BUT IT'S WORTH IT!

SOME QUESTIONS?

#1

"Brother Lovett, about the verse which says . . .

'Likewise ye wives, be in subjection to your own husbands; that, if any obey not THE WORD, they also may be won without THE WORD by the behavior of their wives' (1 Peter 3:1).

. . . does that mean the wife is not supposed to open her mouth about Christ?"

ANSWER: No. More than one godly wife has read this verse and supposed it meant she must avoid all verbal attempts to reach her husband for Christ. But this is **not** the case. The confusion clears when we observe the verse is NOT telling the wife she is to keep silent, but that she is NOT TO PREACH.

She is NOT told to seal her lips, but to avoid giving back to her husband that which he refuses to obey — THE GOS-PEL. The Gospel (Word of God) is always to be presented with AUTHORITY, and it is **authority** which the wife is NOT TO EXERT over her husband. Doing so cancels her sub-mission. In asking her husband to **submit** to the Gospel, **she is exalting herself over him.** Anyone bringing Gospel de-mands upon another, assumes an exalted role (Heb. 7:7).

As far as instructing the wife NOT TO SPEAK AT ALL, this cannot be the meaning. To insist that she NOT let her light shine would be to over-rule Jesus' command. The Apos-tle is simply telling the wife that inasmuch as her husband has set himself to DEFY the Word of God, she is not to turn around and use that very WORD on him. Observe this has to do with GOD'S WORD. She is to use HER WORD. In the Greek this distinction is quite noticeable. In English where we have only one word for "word," the true meaning is veiled.

We are careful in the nutcracker technique to ask the wife NOT to use **THE** Word on her husband. She must not require him to submit to her authority as a preacher. Yet we insist she must not fail to use HER OWN WORD as the means of illuminating her WORKS. That is not preaching. Her words are beamed upon her works — not her husband. Should she fail to do this, her good works will go to waste, bringing no credit to Christ. She will be regarded as a good woman, receiving all the credit herself.

A husband who resists the Gospel is pained by any thought of the Lord. Consequently he veils his eyes to the truth as surely as he would to bright sunlight. He cannot see, because he does **not want to see** the Lord's working in his wife. Until she opens her mouth to declare it, he WON'T SEE. It is her light shed on her work that FORCES her husband to acknowledge Jesus in his home. This is what pressures him to DO SOMETHING about Christ.

When he comes asking about salvation, then it is a different matter. She is no longer obligated to remain silent about the Gospel. Since he is now ready to OBEY THE WORD, the injunction against her is lifted. She may then break Gospel silence to confront him with Christ ALIVE!

"This plan could easily bring trouble to a wife already in a hard situation. Wouldn't it take a pretty strong woman to use these techniques in such a case? Wouldn't it be better for her to settle for the status-quo, making whatever adjustments are needed?"

ANSWER: Surely you have visited other churches. Listen to those cries as the people get down to business with God on prayer-meeting night:

"Lord, I don't want my husband to go to hell!"

"Please Master, my children need a Christian father."

"Oh God, I'm trying to be a good wife, but it is so hard living with an unsaved man!"

"Precious Saviour, won't you save my husband? He's a good man. I can't stand the thought of his facing eternal agony!"

"Dearest Jesus, Oh how I could serve you with all my heart if only you would reach down and save my husband!"

. . . and on and on and on.

It's like that everywhere. Hosts of women cry under this burden of the unequal yoke. They suffer, indeed they suffer. There is anguish, tearing distress of soul, the deepest hurt— and pain. The question is, how much? Enough to do something about it? Are they content to survive perpetual pain, or will they risk a little more to salvage the situation?

Yes, this plan can cause trouble. But what do they have now, paradise? Just the opposite. For many of these women a little more trouble would be but a drop in the bucket. They would gladly bear more if they really believed it would result in bringing their husbands to Christ, or at the very least, get them out from under that awful yoke.

I won't deny that trouble may come. But I hasten to assure any suffering wife, IT'S WORTH IT. Anything worth having carries a price tag. Nothing of real value is cheap. Our free salvation cost God plenty. For some women it will be a matter of taking what they are ALREADY SUFFERING and illuminating it so that it counts. They are already paying the price, but getting nothing for it. The nutcracker technique can take the price they are already paying and secure the salvation of their mates. We shouldn't be so terrified of trouble, most wives with unsaved mates have it anyway.

It is right to ask this question. I am glad to answer it. But please avoid the temptation of using trouble as an EX-CUSE for **not doing anything.**

"When the Scripture says . . .

'the unbelieving husband is sanctified by the wife . . .'

. . . does that mean his salvation is somewhat assured?"

ANSWER: Indeed not. Only that he is set apart for special treatment.

The heathen husband is yoked to another in whom the Spirit of God dwells. He is chained to the truth of Christ — 24 hours a day. A Christian wife becomes God's unique minister whose principal task is serving and maintaining that man as he makes his way through life. True, the wife's role is not that of a preacher, yet it is just as effective. She has a special, on the spot ministry that fits the situation perfectly. There are Gospel techniques which permit the Christian wife to perform a wooing work which matches her role as a submissive wife. She woos with works, illuminated works.

Her wooing works consist of gentleness and kindness toward her husband. She pleases him, but she also pressures him. She keeps Jesus before him, in the sweetest way. She subtly places her husband in the position of having to credit Christ for all the loveliness that fills his home. He must further acknowledge the graciousness in his wife as due to Jesus. Doesn't that sound like special treatment to you.

This is the sense in which the word, "sanctified" is to be applied. It means being set apart for the special treatment just described. Now there are other meanings for this word as it is used in the New Testament, but this is the meaning as it is employed in the verse above. Judas is a scriptural example of this type of sanctification. He lived with the Lord Jesus. Christ was before him continually. He shared His presence, participating in His ministry. He was brought to full awareness of the truth, yet he was never saved. He was completely sanctified in the sense of this verse, yet this sanctification never secured nor guaranteed his salvation. Nor is your husband's salvation guaranteed either.

"Do the principles set forth in the nutcracker technique have other applications?"

ANSWER: Yes. I have reserved them that they might appear in another work, but I will mention how they might fit other situations.

    a.   Consider for example, the husband with an unsaved wife. He uses the technique in reverse. His acts of caring, comforting and cherishing are his WORKS. Each time he serves his wife in some outstanding way . . . "click" . . . he illuminates that work with his LIGHT. She then is faced with the presence and working of the Lord in her home. She is thereby "sanctified" (set apart for special treatment) as explained above.

Such a husband, observing his wife to be tired, might offer to help with the dishes instead of relaxing in his easy chair. As he nuzzles up to relieve her of her apron, he can click on his light:

"Click". . .

"You know dear, the Lord has given me just one wife and He expects me to take good care of her so she will last. You go sit down and I'll do these. The Lord wants you to enjoy being married to a Christian husband."

b. Or we might think of the lad who is newly saved at a Gospel meeting. He is tempted to go right home and start preaching to his parents. Should he? That doesn't always set so well. But he can start explaining how the CHANGES in his life are due to Christ. Let him go to work improving himself in such specifics as cleaning up his room, dressing neatly for meals, or giving **instant obedience** in his chores — and he has WORKS to illuminate:

"Click". . .

"Now that I have accepted Christ and become a Christian, the Lord expects me to work at being a good son to my parents."

See? His LIGHT shines on his works. What parents would not be moved by this? It stabs deeply, it can move people to action.

c. These same principles apply if one is a Christian employee trying to win his boss, or an employer using his position to cultivate employees for Christ. While an expanded application of these truths is scheduled to appear in another work, no Christian should hesitate to make his own application with what he has in hand. A husband with ingenuity could immediately begin reaching his unsaved wife simply by adapting the dialogues of this book to his role. Nothing would please me more than to hear that God's people everywhere are finding ways to fit these truths to their own situations, and squeezing souls for Christ.

"What if I start out with this technique and find I reach a place where I can go no farther? Is it profitable to go only part way, or must one always reach a showdown with her husband before the plan is fully effective?"

ANSWER: No matter how far you go with the plan three things will happen:

(1) Changes occur in you. Even the first steps find you exercising a new kind of self-restraint and personal control. You cannot help but begin to watch your words and their effect on your husband. This has to be healthy.

(2) You learn to involve the Holy Spirit more intimately with your problems. He becomes "instant comfort" in your stress, "instant strength" as you speak to your husband. One of the first benefits is watching His witness accompany your words.

(3) No matter where you halt in the plan, your husband is that much more aware of his perilous condition. The more insight he has to his predicament, the closer he is to the kingdom.

Your goal should be **willingness** to go all the way with the plan if necessary. But if you find you can't, don't despair. Airliners sometimes have to hold over an airport while waiting for weather to clear. You might have to hold at a pressure-level until it appears wise to move on. Don't let Satan arouse frustration within you if that happens. Waiting can be good, it gives time for evaluation of the ground .covered so far.

A nice thing about such a plan is that if you make any progress at all, you are a success. Don't feel bad if circumstances force you to stop. **Involuntary** delays are in God's hands, usually. If you reach a point where further progress appears impossible, praise God for what He has **already** accomplished and be content.

"I'm not suffering too much in my situation. I've learned to live with it. In fact, I think I've made a pretty good adjustment. My husband goes his way, I go mine. Is it really wise for me to upset this nice balance and get involved in a pressure-plan to reach him for Christ? Isn't it better to let sleeping dogs lie?"

ANSWER: You could do that. But please note that one thing has already changed. You have come into possession of a plan for reaching your husband. You have knowledge of what you could do and knowledge brings responsibility. God holds us accountable for what we know. We will be judged for what we do with it. Since you have now read this book, it won't be easy for you to sit back and watch your mate travel the road to hell when you **can do something about it.** It is akin to something Jesus once said:

"If I had not come, they had not known sin. . ."

But He did come. The excuses of the Pharisees were wiped out.

Regardless of any adjustments you might make, that "sanctified" man is your mission field. If you can hold this plan in your hands and feel no responsibility to try it, something is wrong. It is not possible that the Holy Spirit will allow you to be comfortable in such a situation, particularly when He stands ready to help. If you can read this book and do nothing about it, something in you is either dead or will surely die.

TITLES MENTIONED IN THIS BOOK...BY C. S. LOVETT

No. 510 **DEALING WITH THE DEVIL** **$5.95** (hardback, includes FREE ANTI-SATAN KIT) 160 pages, illustrated

No. 523 **DEALING WITH THE DEVIL** **$2.95** (paper, no kit)

No. 201 **SOUL-WINNING MADE EASY** **$1.75** (80 pages, paper)

No. 101 **WITNESSING MADE EASY** **$3.95** (256 pages, paper)

No. 503 **THE COMPASSIONATE SIDE OF DIVORCE** **$3.25**

No. 301 **VISITATION MADE EASY** **$1.75** (80 pages, paperback)

No. 502 **DEATH: GRADUATION TO GLORY** **$2.95** (144 pgs)

No. 107 **YOUR BIGGEST DECISION** Booklet 15¢

additional copies of
No. 516 **UNEQUALLY YOKED WIVES** **$2.95** (160 pages, pb.)

other related titles
No. 504 **"HEAVEN ON EARTH" MARRIAGE CASSETTE**
$4.95 Shaky marriages need the healing power of this intimate 25 min. cassette, narrated by Dr. Lovett. (plastic case)

No. 527 **THE 100% CHRISTIAN** **$2.95** Includes FREE action kit to help you to be a 100% Christian. (128 pages, paper)

No. 537 **JESUS WANTS YOU WELL!** **$3.95** (304 pages, paper)

No. 520 **JESUS IS COMING—GET READY CHRISTIAN!** **$2.95**

(PRICES SUBJECT TO CHANGE)

Available at your local Christian bookstore
or order direct from:

PERSONAL CHRISTIANITY
Box 549, Baldwin Park, California 91706

PERSONAL CHRISTIANITY IS ..

A local church with a literature ministry.

We are incorporated under the Laws of the State of California as a local church.

We not only provide a worship center for the residents of the area, but exist as a "ministry of helps" [1 Cor 12:28] toward the "Body of Christ."

PC is not affiliated with any denomination, organization or council of churches.

God has given PC the task of producing the spiritual mechanics for personal obedience to the Great Commission and maturity in the Christian life. Unique, know-how tools are developed within the church and made available to God's people everywhere. Our outreach is by means of the U.S. Postal system which makes possible *personal contact* with individuals and churches across the land and throughout the world.

We bear the name PERSONAL CHRISTIANITY because we seek to involve people personally with the Lord Jesus, the Holy Spirit and the Great Commission.

All who care about Christ are welcome to worship with us. Those further interested in "equipping Christians for action," are invited to invest their talents and strengths with ours. We are interested in every Christian and church willing to take a vigorous stand for Christ in these gloomy days.

Brother Lovett was saved through his "accidental" attendance at a minister's conference where he eavesdropped the conversation of a group of nationally known Christian leaders. There he overheard a discussion on the mechanics of salvation. For years he had been under conviction, yet no one troubled to introduce him to Christ. Armed with the necessary insight for the salvation experience, he hurried home to share it with his wife, Marjorie.

Together they knelt and invited Christ to come into their hearts.

A graduate of California Baptist Theological Seminary, he holds the M.A. and B.D. degrees conferred Magna Cum Laude. He has completed graduate work in Psychology at Los Angeles State College and holds an honorary doctorate from the Protestant Episcopal University in London. He is a retired Air Force Chaplain with the rank of Lt. Colonel.

Pastor Lovett is the author of the books and tools produced by Personal Christianity. The advent of his "Soul-Winning Made Easy," has dramatically changed evangelism methods in America, while the anti-satan skill offered in his "Dealing with the Devil," has alerted multitudes to their authority over our enemy through Christ. Dr. Lovett's experience as an editor of the Amplified New Testament and a director of the foundation which produced it, prompted him to begin work on "Lovett's Lights on the New Testament." His ability to explain the deep things of God in simple language, allows readers to understand their Bibles as the Holy Spirit intends they should.

NOTES:

NOTES:

NOTES: